RESISTING ARREST

poems to stretch the sky

edited by Tony Medina

North Carolina

Cover & interior design: Daniel Krawiec
Cover photo: *The Return of Trayvon* by Thomas Sayers Ellis

Proceeds from the sales of this book will be donated to the "Whitney M. Young Social Justice Scholarship" sponsored by The Greater Washington Urban League, Thursday Network.

The Greater Washington Urban League Young Professionals Auxiliary - Thursday Network is a 501c3 organization whose mission is *the consistent quest to continue the work of their ancestors by advancing education and economic development, restoring pride, and combating systems of oppression in their communities.*

ISBN 978-0-936481-09-8
Library of Congress Control Number: 2015959674

Jacar Press
6617 Deerview Trail
Durham, NC 27712
www.jacarpress.com

Writing is fighting.

— *Ishmael Reed*

Call Their Names

You can't write poems about the trees
when the woods are full of policemen.
                                    —Bertolt Brecht

The rate at which black and brown—and even white—people killed by police are packing American morgues is breathtaking. The rotting stench of such outlandish policing is enough to lead mobs of people to their local jailhouses and police precincts demanding justice lest they turnover each façade brick by brick.

That would be the ideal scenario. But the reality on the ground is that throngs of concerned citizens in various cities across the country—and even overseas—have taken to the streets to protest the killings of unarmed civilians by police. Even as protestors face down militarized units armed with tanks, teargas, high tech weapons and riot gear, unions and blue brotherhoods of silence, operating with impunity and the full protection of the State, continue to exonerate corrupt cops.

And so the bodies, in the past two years alone, mount.

Sarah Lee Circle Bear, a 24-year-old pregnant South Dakota Lakota woman, jailed on a bond violation, was found dead in a holding cell in Brown County Jail after staff ignored her when she cried out that she was in "excruciating pain." The staff, indifferent to Sarah's physical distress, claimed she was "faking". After finally relenting to inmates' cries to provide medical attention for Sarah Lee Circle Bear, jailers dragged her to a holding cell where she eventually succumbed to her injuries.

Sandra Bland, a 28-year-old African American woman was pulled over in Waller County, Texas. A trooper who roughly took her into custody and who was taped lying on camera about her "kicking him" and resisting arrest had tailed Sandra. Sandra Bland, an outspoken anti-police brutality social media activist, was found less than 48 hours later hanging in a Waller County jail cell.

Though Sandra Bland's tragic altercation with Texas law enforcement garnered a firestorm of public outrage and media attention, Sarah Lee Circle Bear's abuse and senseless death practically went unnoticed in mainstream media, as did Choctow activist Rexdale W. Henry's death (one day after Sandra Bland's) in a Neshoba County Jail cell in Philadelphia, Mississippi after being arrested for a minor traffic citation, highlighting the ongoing erasure and invisibility of American society towards its indigenous peoples and cultures.

Ironically enough, mainstream media was also not too interested in a white life lost to the rash violence of police. Troy Goode, a white 30-year-old father who died in the back of an ambulance after being hogtied by police (his repeated complaints of not being able to breathe ignored), was swept under a virtual rug. Had it not been for young black activists of the burgeoning Black Lives Matter movement who began tweeting news of Troy's death, it would have never received the scant attention in mainstream media it eventually did.

The antagonistic actions against Black Lives Matter has been met with derisive claims that BLM privileges black life over *all* life, which has become not solely a conservative criticism but a liberal kneejerk response to the Black Lives Matter mantra, causing white politicians and some black celebrities alike to tweet or publically pronounce misguided correctives like "All Lives Matter," which not only misses the point of the movement in necessitating the fact that black and brown people are disproportionately profiled, targeted, harassed, brutalized and killed by police—and who suspiciously end up dead while in police custody—but suggests some sort of racial essentialism on the part of BLM activists, cynically attempting, of course, to turn the public against the movement.

But despite the swirl of controversy that surrounds American movements for social change (nothing new), the mounting focus of policing in America reveals an insecurity of late capitalism where people are increasingly warehoused in privatized prisons that have become work camps and Gulags. Beyond the grotesque incarceration rates of black and brown men, more and more women and children of color are ending up behind bars at alarming rates rather than in the workforce or in educational institutions. Our children are exponentially victimized by the judicial system, vacuumed into the prison industry and brutalized and traumatized by the strong arm tactics of American policing that targets them less and less for a future guided by education and its probable path toward success, but incarceration—or death. Black and brown children who exist in a dualism that both erases them and renders them invisible while simultaneously seeing them as adults and *not* children (which is the privilege of white youth), are not—have never been—safe.

Five years ago, in St. Petersburg, Florida, 5-year-old Naisha was hauled off in handcuffs by three cops for having a tantrum at Fairmount Park Elementary School. Two years later, 6-year-old Salecia Johnson who was arrested and handcuffed by Milledgeville, Georgia police after a temper tantrum in the principal's office at Creekside Elementary School. This year, at least two cases came to media attention: in Philadelphia, Connor Ruiz, a 5-year-old special needs child, was handcuffed and shackled in a patrol car for being "combative" while in Irving, Texas, 14-year-old Sudanese Muslim whiz kid, Ahmed Mohamed, was arrested at school and handcuffed by five police officers after his teachers at Irving MacArthur High mistook his homemade clock for a bomb in an act of post-911 Islamophobia.

The sinister collusion of law enforcement and schools in becoming holding pens for prison and spaces in which our children are traumatized is egregious enough. Yet public spaces remain the primary proving ground for their fatal altercations with law enforcement, outside of prisons and detention centers, sadly.

We're not only seeing children being violently handled by police, we're also witnessing the murders of children. In Cleveland, Ohio, 12-year-old Tamir Rice had a pellet gun at the Cudell Recreation Center. He was gunned down by two police officers responding to a dispatch of a "black male sitting on a swing and pointing a gun at people." The officer responding to the dispatcher's call was recorded saying the gun in question was probably a fake and the suspect was most likely a juvenile. It was later reported that one of Tamir's shooters was regarded as "an emotionally unstable recruit" and was considered "unfit for duty".

13-year-old Andy Lopez fared no better than Tamir. He was toting a toy gun in Santa Rosa, California; his resembled an AK-47 assault rifle. A Sonoma County sheriff's deputy spotted Andy walking through a vacant lot and, believing his toy gun to be real, opened fire, fatally wounding him.

Police have behaved with unmitigated force and indifference to citizens' humanity and the number of national incidents of police violence is increasingly transversing communities. Just ask Brooke Fantelli who filed a lawsuit against the U.S. Bureau of Land Management, claiming she was tased by a federal ranger on her crotch that discovered she was a transgender woman after checking her ID.

In Miami two police officers stalked 22-year-old Gilberto Powell because they claimed he had a suspicious bulge in his pants. After striking him and knocking him to the ground, then handcuffing and questioning him, the officers realized he had Down syndrome. They later reported that he was "mentally challenged, was not capable of understanding our commands, and that the bulge in his waistband was a colostomy bag" which had been ripped open during the assault. When he was released into his parents' care, Gilberto's pants were off; and he was only in his boxer's.

It's not hard to understand why Chris Rock videotaped himself being pulled over near his home in an affluent part of New Jersey. He had been pulled over three times in seven weeks, tweeting: "Stopped by the cops again, wish me luck." The officer was trained to be especially suspicious of black men driving expensive vehicles.

An undercover cop in Manhattan tackled former American tennis star James Blake as he waited for a car service. The officer had mistaken him for Sean Satha, who himself was mistaken for another man in a fraud case. The assaulting officer in question has had four other lawsuits lodged at him for other acts of unnecessary use of force. Blake took to social media and stated, "When you police with reckless abandon you need to be held accountable."

Police brutality is more and more becoming a regular occurrence. It seems like police departments would rather face liability (paid for by taxpayers) than spare a black and brown life. What many Americans are realizing is that black and brown skin allows police to kill with impunity, justifying their actions. They seem to operate with a Jim Crow mentality of keeping us in our place, turning us into percussion instruments and human bull's eyes. And when police are repeatedly exonerated—adding insult to injury like pissing on the graves of the slain—we are expected to believe the officer's word over what we are witnessing with our own eyes.

Not even videotaped recordings can convince those conditioned by the magical thinking of white supremacy of police officers' guilt. For we black and brown citizens continue to be colonized by whiteness and privilege that suggests that our lives do not matter, and that we are guilty when police say so; that our very breath is resisting arrest.

The narratives are becoming more Kafkaesque and absurd: handcuffed in the back of a patrol car, he grabbed the officer's gun and shot himself dead in his chest; she hanged herself in her cell with a trash bag; he broke his spine by deliberately careening his body against the steel walls of the police wagon like a pinball while handcuffed and shackled; you did not make your self small enough, invisible enough; you did not prostrate yourself on the ground; you were breathing; you blinked; you were recklessly eyeballing me; you shouldn't have smiled; don't talk back; don't ask questions; I don't care if you do know the law—this gun and badge *trumps* your rights; I thought the wallet was a gun; I thought the child's thumb and forefinger was a gun; the light flashing off her wristwatch resembled a knife; I thought the side-eye she gave me was *actually* a gun; she should've never given me any lip!

Even as atrocities are caught on dashcams, revealing the lie to the world exposing American policing while calling into question our nation's democratic ethos of truth and justice for all, black and brown folks continue to have their blood shed at the hands of sociopaths licensed to kill: Jonathan Ferrell shot 12 times after seeking assistance when his car broke down, 8 of the shots into his back while he was crawling; Walter Scott, fatally shot in the back like a target study as he loped away like a toddler; Sam DuBose shot in the head as he was sitting in his vehicle upon being pulled over by a campus cop for a missing front license; and Gilbert Flores, involved in a domestic disturbance, fatally shot twice in the chest at pointblank range by San Antonio police after raising his arms in surrender.

In the push for police and criminal justice reform some law enforcement agencies have utilized dashboard and body cameras. But some police attempt to fortify themselves against incrimination and litigation by disingenuously yelling repeatedly, "Stop resisting" while apprehending suspects in strangely sinister and cynical acts of covering their asses as they attempt to get away with their gratuitous use of force. In Stockton, California, cops are under fire for arresting a black teen for jaywalking. On camera, the 16-year-old is shown being pummeled in the face by an officer with a baton who is yelling for him to, "Stop resisting! Stop resisting!" It's apparent the teen is not resisting nor does he pose a threat to the 5 hulking officers as they hogtie him. In a similar scenario, rap artist Wiz Khalifa posted a video on Instagram of himself being taken down and handcuffed by police as he was violently arrested for "refusing to get off his personal hoverboard." In the clip, the officers are yelling at Khalifa, "Stop resisting!" while he calmly explains, "I'm not resisting. I'm not resisting, sir."

Police brutality fills us with ill will via the barrel of a gun; via lead hollow tip bullets, via chokeholds and nightsticks and batons raining blood and bone and bits of flesh from our weary heads. And when more and more white Americans are shown to the world to suffer similar fates as Troy Goode and Michael Bell, Jr.—and others even less publicized have—we may see a dramatic paradigm shift in American policing. And maybe that will be our Guernica. But as it stands, American society—and mainstream media—wants us to believe that police brutality is a pigment of our imagination.

Where would media outlets like CNN and MSNBC and FOX be without black and brown bodies sacrificed at the altar of American policing? They love to run the videotaped images into the ground like popcorn porn for the kukluxdontgivesafux. They love to provide a defense for what is clearly the indefensible. They create absurd debates as if killing brown and black people were an academic parlor game. They get off and get rich on exploiting our televised wholesale slaughter. They feel no civic responsibility but to fill airspace with a 24-hour circus show parading those who could care less about our daily horrors, parading the loved ones of the slain into their studios or on Skype only to have them juxtaposed against the inane opinions of pathetic shills for the police, to justify our murder, selling America and the white imagination on the heroism and sacrifice of those charged to carry weapons too readily used against us.

Police killings of citizens of color are becoming an American past time way past its prime. But one thing we can depend on in this hour of chaos, confusion, clarity, outrage and sorrow: America's media will certainly be there to insinuate itself, however crudely, however clumsily and rudely, into the sickness of the American psyche.

No need for me to further enumerate the endless trail of police violations, brutalities, killings. I'll let the poets sing their names. I'll let the Tradition say, *Amen*! For the great and socially committed poets assembled herein have been engaged in call and response; bearing witness to the maladies of a nation whose so-called founding begins with brutality and policing; begins with genocide, confiscation and death in the name of profit, greed and expansion.

The poet-witnesses in this collection distill the horror and let in the light of our common humanity. They remind us of a universal hurt, grief, anger, rage, shame and love that we all can recall when confronting the blunt reality and the savagery of abuses associated with corrupted power, indifference and intolerance.

This is not a catalogue of death and despair. This is a work of resistance and resilience. These poets sing songs of love, which is what this book is, essentially.

Guernica.

— Tony Medina

The Poems

RESISTING ARREST

How We Could Have Lived or Died This Way

Not songs of loyalty alone are these,
But songs of insurrection also,
For I am the sworn poet of every dauntless rebel the world over.

— *Walt Whitman*

I see the dark-skinned bodies falling in the street as their ancestors fell
before the whip and steel, the last blood pooling, the last breath spitting.
I see the immigrant street vendor flashing his wallet to the cops,
shot so many times there are bullet holes in the soles of his feet.
I see the deaf woodcarver and his pocketknife, crossing the street
in front of a cop who yells, then fires. I see the drug raid, the wrong
door kicked in, the minister's heart seizing up. I see the man hawking
a fistful of cigarettes, the cop's chokehold that makes his wheezing
lungs stop wheezing forever. I am in the crowd, at the window,
kneeling beside the body left on the asphalt for hours, covered in a sheet.

I see the suicides: the conga player handcuffed for drumming on the subway,
hanged in the jail cell with his hands cuffed behind him; the suspect leaking
blood from his chest in the back seat of the squad car; the 300-pound boy
said to stampede barehanded into the bullets drilling his forehead.

I see the coroner nodding, the words he types in his report burrowing
into the skin like more bullets. I see the government investigations stacking,
words buzzing on the page, then suffocated as bees suffocate in a jar. I see
the next Black man, fleeing as the fugitive slave once fled the slave-catcher,
shot in the back for a broken tail light. I see the cop handcuff the corpse.

poems to stretch the sky

I see the rebels marching, hands upraised before the riot squads,
faces in bandannas against the tear gas, and I walk beside them unseen.
I see the poets, who will write the songs of insurrection generations unborn
will read or hear a century from now, words that make them wonder
how we could have lived or died this way, how the descendants of slaves
still fled and the descendants of slave-catchers still shot them, how we awoke
every morning without the blood of the dead sweating from every pore.

— Martín Espada

Every 28 Hours

is a story of radiant steam,
rising like a metal jacketed
swarm of hornets,
singeing sight from eyes.
a parabola of lava
moldering down a mountain
igniting all green into gray ash,
the siren song of
a bass hit recorded,
number 1 with a uranium
depleted bullet.

It is not a video camera
at Fruitvale Station,
A series of Tweets from
Ferguson MO,
Or a headline in
A New York City daily.

This is not
about Trayvon Martin,
Michael Brown,
Oscar Grant,
Amadou Diallo,
Sean Bell,
James Byrd Jr.
or <insert black body here>

These are not the strings
Of a "suspicious" hoodie
in the wrong hood
or a guy who shouldn't
have run from the cops,

is not a fable of a corpse
with an eight track
of bullets in its back,
this has never mistaken
its gun for a Taser,
isn't a simple chokehold
takedown gone wrong

This is a story
that checks out,
so the only charges
will be on a credit card
for funereal services.

I did not write this poem
in anger,
I did not write this poem
in "Self-Defense".
I did not write this poem.
Because my pen is empty from
having already written
& re-written this poem.

These words can be heard
only because
while facedown
on the concrete
of the righthand lane
at 10:37 AM
on April 15th, 1987
at 19067 Greenbelt Road
my name was not Gregory Habib,
my sternum
could stand the weight
of the knee between

my shoulder blades,
and the monomaniacal eye
at the back of my head
was a .38 revolver
with a 15 lb. trigger pull
and not the 8 lb pull
of a Glock 9mm.
Because it was all just

a misunderstanding
and have a nice day, Sir.

It is not true that
my eyes are red
as a bag of Skittles
and if my page is dotted
with drops, it is only Arizona
iced tea that spills.

This pertains to no crime,
contains no rough barked trees
with branches strong enough
to bear the kicking
weight of a black boy,
contains no rope (of any length),
contains not even a single slipknot.

But it does loop,
like a wandering moose,
a homeward goose,
or a four hundred year old
ruse.

— Joel Dias-Porter

Congo Square Is Everywhere

Now as we wish for music that went unrecorded,
as we eat under reconstructed magnolias, blind
to brash ways people try to forget sacred music,

in negligence of voices that lived in the souls
of the dead, innermost light in a candle's flame,
diminutive knees bending until the day we refuse

the genuflecting, the failure to see God has moved
the line of action to where we must wear the prayers,
stand up, sing out to where God can feel appreciated,

to where we are honored as human against the power
of thieves, the need some have to prove they own more
than any of us can own, in Congo Square, octaves

above the silence of harvests dying a shrill death
in drought brought on when tears dry and marrow
waits for us to know Congo Square is everywhere.

It breathes, it lives when we refuse brutality.

— Afaa Michael Weaver

elegy

(for MOVE* and Philadelphia)

1.

philadelphia
  a disguised southern city
squatting in the eastern pass of
colleges cathedrals and cowboys.
philadelphia. a phalanx of parsons
and auctioneers
  modern gladiators
erasing the delirium of death from their shields
while houses burn out of control.

2.

c'mon girl hurry on down to osage ave
they're roasting in the fire
smell the dreadlocks and blk/skins
roasting in the fire.

c'mon newsmen and tvmen
hurryondown to osage ave and
when you have chloroformed the city
and after you have stitched up your words
hurry on down for sanctuary
in taverns and corporations

and the blood is not yet dry

3.

how does one scream in thunder?

4.

they are combing the morning for shadows
and screams tongue-tied without faces
look. over there. one eye
escaping from its skin
and our heartbeats slowdown to a drawl
and the kingfisher calls out from his downtown capital
and the pinstriped general reenlists
his tongue for combat
and the police come like twin seasons of drought and flood.
they're combing the city for lifeliberty and
the pursuit of happiness.

5.

how does one city scream in thunder?

6.

hide us O lord
deliver us from our nakedness
exile us from our laughter
give us this day our rest from seduction
peeling us down to our veins.

and the tower was like no other   amen.
and the street escaped under the
cover of darkness   amen.
and the voices called out from
their wounds   amen.
and the fire circumsized the city   amen.

7.

who anointed this city with napalm?   (i say)
who giveth this city in holy infanticide?

8.

beyond the mornings and the afternoons
and deaths detonating the city.
beyond the tourist roadhouses
trading in lobotomies
there is a glimpse of earth
this prodigal earth.
beyond edicts and commandments
commissioned by puritans
there are people
navigating the breath of hurricanes.
beyond concerts and football
and mummuers strutting their
sequined processionals.
there is the earth. This country. this city.
this people.
collecting skeletons from waiting rooms
lying in wait. For honor and peace.
one day.

— Sonia Sanchez

*MOVE: a philadelphia based back to nature group whose head-
quarters was bombed by the police on May 13, 1985, killing men,
women and children. An entire city block was destroyed by fire.

Survival Guide for Animals Born in Captivity

The trick is to get on the ground and fold
yourself into a small, soft shape.

To be in no way
sudden. To smile

but keep your lips
tight shut. The trick is

don't get smart. Don't dream.
Don't imagine. Pull yourself up

but not too up. Don't forget
you don't belong

to anyone or any place at all.
Don't flinch. Don't startle.

The trick is you
were never meant

to be let in. This life
is not for you.

Don't protest.
Don't complain.

The trick is you buck
against your skin.

The boys look like men and the girls
get exactly what they want.

Surrender.
Deserve it.

The trick is your body itself
is a violence. This is all your fault.

— Camille Rankine

Look Back in Hatred

There's a film poster with the title "don't look back in hatred"
On it the profile of youngish Black man, distressed?

Who knows what the story is, but the title's admonition
Makes me ask; why not look back in hatred?
There are situations, people who deserve ire.

They grab all the money, land, power.
They kill your sister or your mother.
They try to kill you.

They kill your brother or your father
They try to kill you.

What better emotion to fit the response to
The situation, the person, the time.

But maybe our youngish Black man has moved on.
Filled his heart with compassion. Learn to trust
Come into the circle of kindness and wants
Never to leave. Good for him. But

What of the situation, the person, the time?
Where is justice? Who will stand accused?
And be judged? How will the law's slow
Reach find the killers, the exploiters, the vicious ones?

Don't look back in hatred. We desire peace.
Harmony, yet, why not demand Justice?

I'd go see a movie call *Demanding Justice*.
I go see a movie about a real Django
Who joins up with John Brown's Anti-Slavery
Brigade brandishing weapons and singing freedom.

A movie about a man whose heart has been whipped
Whose cries are heard by birds and crickets

A man whose hands have been broken
Oh how he
Avenges the blasted hopes his body has

Carved in slow motion. In quick anger
In the tongues loosened only by drink
And fear. That man can stand with his hatred
Mark its shape. Watch a ventriloquist

Tell the dummy's tale- bracing
Conjurer of numbers, locations, shifts in electricity

The man who looks back in hatred and sees
With gratitude the opportunity to smash
That dummy's blank
Face.

And the man's hand hods splinters from the touch
Of a wood so hard, it must be endangered.

— Patricia Spears Jones

Strangled*: Letter to a Young Black Poet

for D. A.

A zombie is a technological soldier
ingrained in race
trying the spirits of beautiful folks like you.
A zombie moves in the same moment wrong
together with other zombies sluggish,
the apex of not feeling.
This is all to say: you are not a zombie.
Wash, rinse, repeat.
You are not a zombie.
You are tired.
What you feel is valid.
Speak this insane ass country.
Slap the shit out of privileged spaces.
Study the hiatus of hermits.
Be a moving arbor, thankful.
Meet the words of loving others.
Understand respect is not love.
Work through talking rage.
Weep blocks of wood.
Live.
This is all to say #blackpoets love you.
#blackpoestspeakout to and for you.
This is all to say I myself love you.
Wash, rinse, repeat.
I love myself loving you.
Soon.
Breathe

      Breathe
          Breathe

poems to stretch the sky

*All words taken from D.A.'s Facebook post about the energy it takes to exist in predominantly White spaces, posted November 28, 2014.

— Rae Paris

Sometimes I Get So Worried

Sometimes I get so worried,
it is hard to breathe. Even today,
when the sun suddenly appears and lights
the world with magic after all
these weeks of snow and bleakness,

I am ashamed of everything we've done
to destroy the incredible beauty of the earth,
the global warming people still claim
is not caused by our actions, because—
look how cold it has gotten, all the snow
even in Georgia and Tennessee,
the south, flummoxed by icy roads,
my friend says that proves
that global warming is a liberal hoax,
and I do not want to argue but I want to say
when did ignorance become a virtue,
science and facts disputed by people
who do not believe anything
that they don't want to believe.

Congressmen talk about putting more boots
on the ground in the Middle East,
and they seem to ignore that the boots
will not be empty, but instead
will be worn by young people who will die,
because these people love war,
as though they were still children
playing with toy guns
and making shooting noises.

I am so worried I cannot breathe.
Where is the America I grew up
believing in, everything we do now
seems designed to destroy it, a crack
opening down the middle of the country,
too many young men killed by police,
the names a litany of grief—Michael Brown,
Eric Garner, Tamir Rice, Freddie Gray,

Sometimes I get so worried
it is hard to breathe.

— Maria Mazziotti Gillan

Citation, or Safe in Bed-Stuy

Maybe it was the absurd sight of a helmeted man
pissing on a fence. Maybe, that it was a fence
separating the sidewalk from a playground. Maybe
it was because it was 4AM and everything wrong
happens at 4 in the morning – every dumb story
every fight that ended the night at the club
when I was young and these streets not yet
worth policing. But the bright eyed fresh cop
boy sliding up to say *Hey buddy*, must not recognize
I'm twice his age, or that I have my dick
in my hand. Maybe he and his partner haven't yet
processed the sleek, white-wheeled, bullhorn-handled
bicycle leaned up next to me, before he asks
the next dumb-ass question – *didn't you see us there?*
And for two seconds my drunk brain is aflight with
all the unsmart things I want to say
-Yeah I saw you, I wanted to show you my dick.
-Nah, I didn't, but I sure am glad you're here now.
- Yeah I actually was trying to piss on your shoes but I'm too drunk
            to aim right,
but only the self-preservation me speaks
- Uhm, no. Of course not.

But the pig won't relent. He's got a treasure trove
of questions like these he saves for 4AM, for
grown black men on Quincy Street,
Bedford-Stuyvesant on the come up
hood type joint while he hoofs
his beat. *You couldn't hold it, huh?*
And I'm worried that there might
be a little smile on my face now – 19
year old wise-ass me showing up late
with cocaine and tequila to fuck the party
up. *No,* I say. *I just couldn't.*

And he and his partner are so not yet
old enough to legally get the kind of drunk
I am right now, but they're one thumb

poems to stretch the sky

nonchalant in a belt, one hand casual
on a service revolver type sure of themselves –
and the one barks something into his radio
and is oinking something about how he could
give me a much worse citation but he'll let me get off
easy, *but you shouldn't pee in public* blah blah blah
like I ain't been potty trained several years before
his parents even thought to fuck each other.

And the couple that passes by just then, not even
noticing the commotion shouldn't need to enter
the poem except just ten years ago, the police
wouldn't be walking the beat here – just cruising
by in squad cars and asking my purple haired
combat boot girlfriend if she was sure she was
in the right place. But tonight that cop is just
as sure the tittering blondes passing just behind him
are safe because he's got this under control.

And then, almost silently, a murmuring among them
like a group of Jesuits on the way to mass, ten more
police show up, their shoes not making a sound
and they stand around while babyface runs my ID
and I'm thinking that isn't it something, this is really
how it's gonna go down, beat to death by cops
in Bed-Stuy or maybe my life saved by my bicycle
helmet like everyone always says it would, and my
little girl in her mother's belly still, will never meet
me. So I try to hold the gaze of the one black cop,
a woman, young, and hope she sees her brother
standing here, or her man, or her father. But she
looks everywhere except my face, and her thumb
is tucked in her belt too, and her hand, resting on
the 9mm like an afterthought, all of them doing
their jobs, polite and casual – in Bed-Stuy, finally
to protect, to serve.

— Roger Bonair-Agard

Two Meditations On Walter Scott

(i)
Future Tense

I think you will let me run, you will follow walking
at a brisk pace, soon I will be out of breath,
soon the pain in my ankle and knees will slow me,
soon there will be a fence between me and escape,
soon I will wonder about my heart, and you
who know my name, you who can see my body's distress
will chuckle softly, watching me sit, watching me saying
Okay, okay, okay, you got me—and maybe we will
laugh, and you will say, *Man you need to lose some.*

And I will roll on my stomach and welcome the soft
damp cool of the grass, and you will then put on
the cuffs, and I will say, *Not so tight,* and you will say
How's that?, and I will say, *Thanks, and sorry man,
just got freaked by the Taser,* and you will say,
You know that was some stupid shit you pulled,
and I will say, *Yeah man, sorry,* and you will say
I could have shot you, and something about being
pissed off and all the dammed paperwork,
and even though I will want to I won't say,
All this over a broken tail light?!, or,
You know you wrong to stop me, but instead I will say
I used to run better, and you will say, *Football?,*
And I will say, *Yeah, we get fat after a while,*
and then the sirens of the back up will fill the air,
and my heart will sink, but will still be beating
and that will be the end of the day, see?

How optimistic and forgiving of me to cast this all
in the future tense, as if I have some dream that someday
this is how a Blackman and a white cop will laugh
on a sunny Charleston afternoon; how forgiving
of me to avoid the judgment of the subjunctive,
of the abstracted hope of what might have been,
when we know that what has been

is an indictment of what might have been.
Old sinner man, where yuh gonna run to
downpressorman where yuh gonna run to,
on that day, on that day, on that day?

So you know, I ran from you. I will run from you,
I would run from you because I grow stupid
when I am around you, and you might ask me
who you is and all I can say is you is not me,
which is never enough, but we are talking about
what has been or what is to come or what should have,
which is another way of saying we can't do a thing
about any of it except to know you is not me.

(ii)
Grief

He is fifty.

I had another thing to say,
then I saw what I have sought not to see,
and it is all that stains my head's insides,
it interrupts the comforts of our bouncing,
leaves me with the endless song of grief.

He is a big man.

He wears black trousers.

He runs like someone who used to run.

He falls like an after thought.

And dying looks so ordinary.

The man with the gun
shoots eight times,
says nothing,
shouts nothing.

Four in the back,
one through the ear.

He was fifty.
He was a big man.
He looked better in black.
His daughter picked out the blue shirt.
My daughter wants me to wear color.

He ran like a man afraid
of the man who has said he was afraid.

He ran then fell like an after thought

The path is ordinary,
the South Carolina green is familiar,
you can feel the soft humidity in the air..

We die easily.

I once read Sir Walter Scott,
the stumbler, the limping one.
But he righted himself,
righted himself.
He did not fall to his face.

Two weeks ago, Nikky
wrote of the wisteria in bloom,
those purple clusters
of southern decorum,
of the season changing.
And when she said. "wisteria"
I thought of the dogwoods,
their leprosy of stoic white
as if cast there to decorate
the new season—those delights,

Those were my rituals of Easter
in Carolina all those years.

It is true that what I see
behind that mute tableau,
the dumb show of bodies
turning violent death
into something mundane,
is the purple pleasure
of wisteria, and a canopy
of dogwood leaves, snow white
in warm Charlestonian April—

I have stopped looking
at the crude obscenity of this,
So these colors, plus the green,
the black, the blue, the pink—
they stain the insides of my head..

We die like animals.
I can't continue tonight
as if this has not happened:

Me running.

Me stumbling.

I am fifty-three.

Perhaps I am wiser.

This is how we grieve strangers.
We grieve selfishly.
We grieve our fear.
We grieve ourselves.
We grieve our grief.
We grieve our grievances.
We grieve the things bigger than grief.
We grieve the way things are.
And maybe old Walter is lost in our grief,
and that, too, is what they stole from him.
They stole his grief.

— Kwame Dawes

All It Took Was Two-and-a-half Seconds

Two-and-a-half seconds for one of the bullets
to pierce a driver's side window and enter
the left side of Danielle Willard's head.

Two-and-a-half seconds for West Valley City police
officer, Shaun Cowley, to access what he perceived
as a threat, pull out 9mm Glock pistol
from his holster and fire three shots.
Two-and-a-half seconds.

"The shooting cost me everything," Cowley says.
"You make a split second decision about whether
you go home that day and someone else does not."
He says he shot Willard because he thought
she would run him over in her Subaru Forester.

Police use of deadly force has been under
a national microscope since the killing
by Officer Darren Wilson of unarmed
Michael Brown in Ferguson, Missouri.
In Cowley's case, race is not an issue
as he is white and so is Willard.
Cowley and his partner were staking out
a house during a drug operation.
One of the suspected drug dealers came out
of the house, got into Willard's car, and got out
a few minutes later. The officers thought
he was ingesting heroin. They approached
the car but she locked it and rolled up
the window. The car was running and she put
her hand on the gearshift, so Cowley thought
she was planning to flee. He ran to his car to get
a crowbar to break the window of her car,

but she started backing up very fast toward him.
He thought she was going to run him over.
Cowley does not remember grabbing his gun,
but he does remember firing it.

Willard was pronounced dead
at the scene. The prosecutor investigated
and said the shooting was not justified.
Police investigating the shooting found
sealed evidence bags in the trunk
of Cowley's car, evidence he had not logged in
or stored properly. It led to an internal audit
of the narcotics unit that found the mishandling
of evidence. Accusations of stolen drugs
and missing money. The narcotics unit
was disbanded and the chief resigned.
Cowley says he did nothing wrong and was
a scapegoat for problems within the narcotics unit.
The case against Cowley was dismissed,
the judge stating the evidence did not show
that Cowley acted recklessly. Cowley was fired.
Today, he is trying to get his job back. He works
with a firm that sells medical equipment.
As he tries to repair his life, he carries
the burden of everything he did
in two-and-a-half seconds.

From an article in the Press and Sun-Bulletin,
Binghamton, NY, Sunday, March 22, 2015

— Maria Mazziotti Gillan

Animals

We're treated like savages
Put in shackles, locked in cages

My fur dark and nappy
Brown skin, black eyes
Round nose, bred by Babylonian
Brothers and savage sisters
Thrashed so I could live peacefully

I'm 17
Dream of going to college
Pursuit of cute girls and knowledge
How can I be comfortable
Leaving my home
Like I'm breaking the law
Wherever I go

Martese on the honor roll
Not allowed to make a mistake
Tried to walk into a bar
Fake ID, face forced to pavement

The color of his skin a condition
An imposition to harm without provocation

We are cannibals, we
Eat each other alive, we
Put each other in cages,we
Watch ourselves
Rot and die

— Nile Lansana

it's hard out here for a spirit

it's hard out here for a spirit.
just trying to settle for
some stability in the gristle marrow
bone tendon muscle warm plasma
of an unarmed black body
on an american street.
i keep getting dislodged as fast
as i used to get chased from the core
of strange fruit.
barely made ten years we
hadn't even finished the fourth grade
when i had to fly away
from clifford glover
on new york boulevard
in spring '73.
he was only ninety pounds but
we did indeed get along.
die little bastard said the killer cops
to my host as i wafted away
a diaphanous dirge.
been mostly riding the wind ever since.
tried to land on the ground in florida
stand on the corner of bay street
and chokehold boulevard
got mistaken for a demon on canfield drive
flashed like a camera's light
through more than half the states in the union.
this frequent flying is overly stressful
because i'm one who would chill
if they didn't keep chilling my people.
it's hard to find time to communicate
anymore or pursue other lofty ideals
so pressed am i to find a home
in blissful blood that can matter.
wish me luck.

— Keith Gilyard

"When Snow Turns to Rain and It Is Still Winter"

I am a Bedouin woman. The goats graze lazily along red stone.
     My gaze.
He was a cheerful boy, my son the poet, grew tall like the poplar with
eyes fiery as embers. My burka weighs and drags. My son

I mutter, as if he had just left the room, the scent of his soap
lingering. My son I start each conversation as though my heart
were whole as a pomegranate clinging to its branch, alive. My son
 writes verses and lives like a monk among hyenas.
He prays, meditates. Say it. My son

Locked behind walls. I once climbed the jagged hills of Petra
hid within its caves. My son sleeps on a pissed stained bunk, once a boy
who had a warm bed, milk, the breast of his mother upon
which to rest his head.

He read books and played with other children.
On the phone now men are loud and he shouts, Ma.   My son.

Each bead I pray upon at dawn has his name. My lips murmur,
God in your heaven.   The chitterling of birds, the desert floor—
     all the same. Why
does the world not long for him as I ? God made us strong this thing
called Mother. The rain and torrents are Mary's tears that cleanse
     the weary. My son
soon my eyes will be illuminated with your presence.

11/17/12

— Ana Castillo

The Talk

It's more than time we had that talk
about what to say and where to walk,
how to act and how to strive,
how to be upright and stay alive.
How to live and how to learn,
how to dig and be dug in return.

When to concede and when to risk,
how to handle Stop and Frisk:
Keep your hands where they can see
and don't reach for your ID
until they request it quite clearly.
Speak to them politely and answer them sincerely.
The law varies according to where you are,
whether you're traveling by foot or driving a car.
It won't help to be black and proud,
nor will you be safer in a crowd.
Keeping your speech calm and restrained,
ask if in fact you're being detained.
If the answer is no, you're free to go.
If the answer is yes, remained unfazed
to avoid being choked, shot or Tased.
Give every cop your ear, but none your wit;
don't tempt him to fold, spindle, mutilate, hit
or otherwise cause pain
to tendons, bones, muscles, brain.
These are things you need to know
if you want to safely come and go.
But still there is no guarantee
that you will make it home to me.
Despite all our care and labor,
you might frighten a cop or neighbor
whose gun sends you to eternal sleep,
proving life's unfair and talk is cheap.

— Jabari Asim

Mother to Son. 2015. Baltimore.

April 28, 2015 at 6:28pm

We won't know why she
snatched at his shirt
tried to hold his lean body back
like burst dam water
served backhand after backhand
across her masked son's head.

Maybe she was trying to change his mind.

Maybe all she had left
when her words ran out
was this smack of action.
Maybe her heart is a charred city,
charmed city.
Her son, her last ember.
We take her footage into our
eyes and mouths, add our own
soundtrack and lean political.

All I see is Sethe,
Margaret Garner,
my mother
and black mothers
who wield love and
the fear of death
like a desperate goddess

— Derrick Weston Brown

Sleepless Ocean

Because you were born a crumbling mountain
Because they made a song in God's throat
Called it   Motown   Called it   Black woman
Called it   "what cannot be killed"

Because babies call you mama mammy nanny
Because the black on your skin sings a lemon bath siren
Because no one asks if it hurts to be this Black
Because no one asks if it hurts to be this kind of woman
Because woman and Black mean silent mean invisible
Because you goin' fight for her babies before your own
Because you know they goin' kill your babies

Because Khadiatou Diallo
Because Lesley McSpadden
Because Sybrina Fulton
Because Valerie Bell
Because Mamie Till

Because a Black mother know ain't no song for that empty in ya belly
Because a Black mother know ain't no ocean big enough to carry
away the corpses

Because you moan
Because you howl
Because you howl
Because you howllll   llllll   llllll   llllll
Because you know the belly croon a ravenous song
Because the sound call the babies back home

Because you home
Because you home
H o m e you be
      Cause you sleep w/your hands thrashing
A lemon wedge beneath the bed frame to keep away an orchestra
     of ghosts

Because Khadiatou Diallo
Because Lesley McSpadden
Because Sybrina Fulton
Because Valerie Bell
Because Mamie Till
Because your Black mother's heart be home to a sleepless ocean
     & even the moon shut it's mouth *tight*   to listen

— Mahogany L. Browne

Unsung

What to make of this growing sorority?
This kinship of sorrow? Mothers of unsung
daughters killed by police, mourning

baby girls in rooms unfazed by sudden
death, where memory won't die but leans
back in an empty chair, fusses in a bathroom

mirror, kicks off her shoes, or naps
on the sofa to never wake, forever 7,
forever asleep, or hangs out in an alleyway

with friends, voluminous laughter bounces
along the walls still, rain logged teddy bears
sag toward the ground, tattered ribbons blow

away with the wind, or splays in the doorway
where she last stood, giving up without a fight,
where each subsequent sweep & mop,

the threshold spills more blood, the floorboards,
the doorjambs, the splattered walls, or rolls around
in a hoopdie with a turbulent engine heard halfway

down the block that will never pull up to the house
again, every beat & throb of the speakers a reminder
of a home now silent, every profanity an endless

raging scream, every night a memorial no one else
attends, every day another death, another restrained
& choked unconscious, another tased to breathlessness,

another trapped in the maze of her own mind abruptly
put at ease, another ride-or-die come true, another old
lady behind on rent, refusing to pay for freezing pipes,

a toilet that won't flush, a warm fridge, evicted
without mercy in a hail of gunfire, another executed
holding a son not even two, another gunned down

in a no-knock on the wrong door, another hanging
after three days in jail for a minor traffic stop. Chant
their names in the streets. Hold them in your vigils.

Count them among the lives that matter.

— Venus Thrash

Black Girls

for Hadiya

when black girls are killed
sometimes
the sky opens
but mostly there is quiet
unless they die in groups
maybe like addie mae, denice, carole and cynthia
who died in 16th street baptist
in sunday school
with starched dresses
and Jesus
but mostly brown girls die everywhere
like juarez's maquiladoras and chicago playgrounds
didn't you know
black girls get murdered before the weather report
on the news but not
after sports
and never on nancy grace's
crusade for justice
or dateline tv special reports
because their boyfriends are bangers
even if they are not?
we cry
and what good is that?
it hurts
but well, life hurts right?
and then your twelve year old
daughter whose skin is gold
says all this murder
makes it hard to plan for the future
mama..like you may not make it to
be a woman..

and you stop her before the rest
before she can finish..
you will live, you say.
she knows this is a command
and she won't disobey you
because you are her mother
who knows what happens
to black girls. but you don't tell
her of all the black women who have been killed
over nothing , just nothing
and so
you won't tell her today. not
today.

— Kelly Norman Ellis

Realism: a poetics

Imagination! who can sing thy force
                    —Phillis Wheatley

The woman's fingers are alternately
two praying mantes in mid fight alternately
the skittish legs of a rock crab blue
limbs swishing left and back to blue
mirages of packed sand untrammeled hole
Free No life forms penetrating the small world a hole
waiting to be dug or alternately
the world is a giant fissure of blue
music classical notes plinking hole
after hole into A Theory of What—
What does the mantis pray for What
does the crab skirt from What
is this life   A force of   What
will happen to this child
I imagine living with me with its child
thoughts and its innocent ways naïve
untouched Is that naïve
to think a child I could birth
untouched by the world before its birth
I think I want to at the least imagine
that tiny world is somewhere I can imagine
many days with this naïve child
its kewpie face a successful imagined birth
It gets hard I will not lie to you
to keep it up The dream I will not lie to you
is hard to keep up Where in this world can I have safe
babies Not me not my love we can not have babies safe
in this world   The woman's fingers are sometimes
praying and prayer is a fight a flight Sometimes

I resent this blond child and her blondish mother
and I hate this resentment but god this mother
imagines a safe world for her daughter
and she will be granted it Her daughter
is a safe world I can only imagine
God I grow weary of the imagination

— Metta Sáma

Police State/ment

From poltergeist to polecat
pottage to police
functionaries of dis order
foam legislation cat call citation
Where anything that moves
or doesn't grace the crosshairs
that triggers the cuffs
It's the old cops and robbers' routine
the cowboys vs Indians shtick
PR on TV subliminally sewn
Slight of hand—knot necessary

Like I scribe to you
I was snagged
by badge glimmer
by industrial strength blue
From bleach to bench in front
of that blind goddess with gauze covered eyes

Lately I've become a mind reader
and tire of this clairvoyant knowing
Can see into the visors
Can recognize the Knights of Empire
rollers on the street
How difficult restraint has become

Dispensers of paddy wagons
projective decrees
My whole life they have been my legacy
Like a dog, I need to shake these fleas off

— T.J. Anderson, III

For Freddie Gray

I've broken
 my heart—
Arm—
And two
Fingers,
(The joy of football)

But never my own
spine.

If I ever need help
With that,

I know who to call.

— Reuben Jackson

Evidence

A Meditation on Race, Police Brutality, and the Power of Assumption

I.

Because, yes, there are good police officers in the world and you have seen them be good. The influx of online battle cries against the police anger you as they seem to go out of their way to ignore the root of the problem: there are too many criminals in the street and those criminals are mostly Black.

You believe that police have the right to be paranoid, extra cautious, trigger- happy when dealing with most people of color because of what you know is their tendency to be criminals. You hear stories, or you don't, about the Black college professor who was pulled over and humiliated for an hour before being let go without even a citation and you think "But he fit the profile," when people of color, in particular Blacks, always fit the profile. Even when they do not fit the profile they fit the profile. You also feel bad for the college professor. He's not one of the bad ones, meaning his career of choice makes him more civilized than the blue collar worker and the thug. Meaning, although he fit the profile it is unlikely that he is indeed the person in the profile because he is a professor and therefore respectable. You feel good about this form of logic. Thus, you are driven to petition: "Not all police! Many are doing the good work!" but the battle cries have fists, have keyboards louder than yours. They have names like AfrikanFreedom, Revolution_INI, and Jake. Their thumbnail photos terrify you. You are so easily terrified.

II.

You ask questions that you feel are important: "What about the thugs, Black and white?" As you type this the idea of a white thug baffles even you but you carry on meaning criminal, meaning that misanthropes come in all colors. You pay no attention to the absence of other races and ethnic groups as potential thugs.

You later type, "Criminals get the law handed to them. End of the discussion." And Michael Brown allegedly fighting that police officer and actually robbing that store of cigarillos means he deserved his death on the streets. Hands in the air. Don't shoot. The media has made up its and your mind.

You ask "Why are they looting and destroying their own communities?" and Rev. Martin Luther King Jr. answers in this excerpt from a longer speech, "The Other America":

"I'm absolutely convinced that a riot merely intensifies the fears of the white community while relieving the guilt[...]But it is not enough for me to stand before you tonight and condemn riots. It would be morally irresponsible for me to do that without, at the same time, condemning the contingent, intolerable conditions that exist in our society [...] And I must say tonight that a riot is the language of the unheard. And what is it America has failed to hear?"

III.

"Officer Wilson deserves his freedom. Pray for peace! Support the police!" The mostly white protesters in St. Louis raised money for defense funds for the officer who shot Brown. They do not have signs that pray for Brown's family because his family is as criminal as they believe Brown to be. Families of criminals do not deserve prayer. The protesters cannot relate to Brown or his family. They see him as a thug, which is the new n-word, which is why there are no white thugs only white "thugs", meaning the misunderstood, the population that has the right to a trial and mental illness as defense. After shooting but before executing Brown, Wilson had the opportunity to call for an ambulance and discontinue shooting. He did not stop shooting. He did not call for an ambulance. He was protecting his life. He was afraid. He was so easily frightened. And only his fears matter as Brown's body was left in the middle of the street as a warning to others that their fear is not credible, that they should get used to seeing this. The protesters in St. Louis would not protest for the officer if the victim was white, meaning if Brown was white he would be alive for due process. We have the past as precedent, as evidence.

poems to stretch the sky

IV.

Because Black-on-Black crime is the mythology of the ages, as though when white people kill other white people it is simply human on human crime, default person on default person crime, and therefore the mentioning of race is unnecessary because these are people after all. Humans. Some people want to identify people by color when it is most convenient to their grasp and maintenance of power, to statements and beliefs that are falsely considered self-evident solely by means of what is visually different. This is not called "playing the race card" though it is the card that, when played centuries ago, created the very concept of race.

Poet Malcolm London debunks Black-on-Black crime swiftly and intelligently here.

V.

You think "he had it coming" because you saw the menace in the boy's face as you've seen the menace in all their faces, the constant anger, the refusal to smile, the inability to make you feel safe. You do not know that many Blacks do not feel safe around white people. You believe in justice and chuckle at the sound play of the Facebook posts, the Tweets coming in by the droves: "justice=just us=just them". And some of your white friends have used the words "animal" and "criminals" for the rioters meaning everyone who rallied but not the police in sniper position. The white friends you have that support Brown's family confuse you but you do not say it. You feel somehow betrayed.

When Jamal in maintenance is arrested, Jamal with whom you've had friendly banter; or Ms. Avery is caught on tape being punched in the face by someone for whom her taxes pay their salary, Ms. Avery the professor/doctor/lawyer/mother/homeless woman; or Tashawna, her name so complicated to say, is maced for no reason—do they get the luxury of being "unfortunate"? Something about their behavior must have warranted the abuse. They must have resisted, though one mustn't resist. And seeing them forcibly handled, restrained, and shaded by a city's, a state's, a nation's indifference comforts you. You are so easily comforted.

VI.

There are good police. In the bastion of good deeds police officers rank highly. Which is why they are held to higher standards as their moral inclination, once debilitated, further debilitates those they serve. It hurts much more when the law blatantly fails because its failure holds such high stakes. Imagine—can you? You are in a town where people look like you and only like you. There is little to no diversity but it is the sign of the times. It is the 1920s, 30s, 40s.

It is Chicago in the year 2014, Lakeview VS Humboldt Park or Englewood VS Wicker Park.

It is St. Louis in the year 2014, the city's train system more a demarcation of segregation than a way to mend segregation.

And in your segregated town there are businesses owned by people who look like you and only like you. You have a bustling economy and education system. Then someone who does not look like you brings in a bunch of people who looks like him or her and they burn your town down. When you look up from the fire, the absolute chaos and ruin, you see the police helping the intruders who have deemed it rightful to destroy everyone's everything because of allegations that one of your own has assaulted one of their own and they want justice: lynching. You do not give up your neighbor to be lynched. So you are destroyed from the ground and the air, the National Guard rallying you all together and putting you in prison camps. Nothing for 32 blocks remains of your town but smoke and char of looted buildings. But this is not what justice is supposed to look like: trial-less, violent, one-sided. This is Greenwood, Tulsa, OK 1921. This is one of many throughout the decades that form the United States of America's history. "But there are good police," you type again in the blog. But can you imagine? Can you?

VII.

You leave a comment on an article about racial profiling "But white people get harassed by police, too. This isn't about…" then stop yourself because the word "race" brings a certain level of engagement that you do not enjoy. You Google links instead, looking for police brutality cases against white people. You find dozens and that is your psychological, emotional, and physical proof. Videos all over Youtube like struck gold for which you could never have enough hands to gather. Documentation. But what you do not notice is the silence after many of these cases of police brutality against whites. You do not notice the dearth of parades and petitions. You do not notice how whiteness has protected white cops even from white citizens. When you ask on the blog "Why don't Black and Latino people ever march for anyone but themselves?" you are silently asking "Where are the white people protesting their own abuses by the hands of the city, state, and nation?" You never think to ask white people this question. You never think of white people as a race and how white silence, its self-appointed default setting, has everything to do with race. And just when you are about to ask why "white" is not capitalized in this piece but "Black" is, the prior sentence hits you. Or it doesn't.

Coda.

You are reading this and thinking "But this is not me" yet still feel indicted though you know this is not you. But this is written to a *you* and if this *you* is not you then why do you feel like you are the *you* referenced here? If you are not the *you* here then why are you relating to the *you* here? Is it a "secret you" that you've kept so well-hidden from yourself? The *you* is floating and does not ask you to catch it; but if you have caught it, are holding it now, have you also given it your name?

— Phillip B. Williams

illustrated equation no. 1

something about a look... something about seeing...

don't

s h o o t

— giovanni singleton

from "The Interrogation"

VI. Multiple-Choice

Metal makes for a chemical reaction.
Now that my wrists are cuffed, I am
                    Not like a citizen. What touches me
                    Claims contamination. What
A shame. A sham. When the police come
They come in steel boots. Precious
                    Metal. They want me kicked,
                    So kick me they do. I cannot say
They love me. But don't they seek me out
As a lover would, each with both hands
                    Bringing me to my knees, under God,
                    Indivisible? I did not have to be born
Here. Men in every nation pray
And some standing and some flat
                    On their backs. Pray luscious
                    Silver. Pray Christmas. A chain
A chain. Even if it's pretty. Even around
The neck. I cannot say what they love
                    Is me with a fist in my new bald mouth.
                    Pray platinum teeth. Show me
A man who tells his children
The police will protect them,
                    And I'll show you the son of a man
                    Who taught his children where
To dig. Not me. Couldn't be. Not
On my knees. No citizen begs
        To find anything other than forgiveness.

poems to stretch the sky

VII. Landmark

What Angel of Death flies by each house, waving

My brother's soul in front of windows like a toy—

A masked, muscle-bound action figure with fists

We wanted when we were children—some light

Item, a hero our family could never afford?

— Jericho Brown

Manifesto of Shame

1. I refuse you. Your blank and arrogant face. Your armor (mis-read your light body). Your dare and follow-through. Disgraceful pain, compressed bullet.

2. Consider one who won't be named. Image shut before become ghost. Ghost before life-eater. Life- eating produce Facebook status. Headline cross passageway – tiny handheld frame boards plane to USA. No image, no body count.

3. Trigger warning: at least one year earlier, C tells me of an uncle (*white*, my emphasis) she has lost. 1991 University of Iowa shooting. A graduate student (Chinese) shoots C's uncle and the other dissertation committee members (all *white*), another graduate student (Chinese), the university's grievance officer (*white*) and Miya (Filipina), a temporary student employee paralyzed from the neck down. Himself. Jo Ann Beard's essay surfaces in the 1997 *Best American Essays*. The university's composition program where I am enrolled teaches this essay in the year when C confesses about the killings. Two films, two non-fiction books. I watch Meryl Streep play a wealthy donor (*white*, obviously) fascinated by culture (Chinese?) who tries to connect with the on-screen shooter. I watch the documentary film about the rest of Miya's life, the ostensible lone survivor become disability advocate. Two films with C – hold her 14 years later. On the plane hearing about this latest outbreak, I call because she has said that mass shootings trigger. No one answers.

4. I do not belong to this chorus. I sit in the grooves of my fractures, put misshapen gun on table. Nobody sees what take shape in room, what force drive into place. Demanding coherence a violent act.

5. I do not want their bones or their bodies. Seung-Hui Cho. Kimveer Gill. One L. Goh. Biswanath Halder. James Jay Lee. Wayne Lo. Gang Lu. Nidal Malik Hasan. Phu Cuong Ta. Jiverly Antares Wong.

6. Not elegy, but fear song. Not praise poem, but a melody of discomfort. What agent causes itchy skin not rest. Pages and pages of small minutes belong to who kill, who monster march forward in time, illegible.

7. To read the shooter (stabber) not as he desired (white, elite) in all shame, but:

Fierce article summarize (our community's) investment in misogylinity, Asian American men's reaction to emasculation. To glorify sexual conquest. To expect access. 31 likes, 22 shares.

I feel useful, attached to my social media. Vigilant against erroneous headlines.

8. I name the ones (some footnotes and predecessors, some spotlights and terrors, deranged enigmas). I am not a victim, but I feel pain.

9. From Murderpedia: Ryan Clark (22) / Emily Hilscher (19) / Minal Panchal (26) / G. V. Loganathan (53) / Jarrett Lane (22) / Brian Bluhm (25) / Matthew Gwaltney (24) / Jeremy Herbstritt (27) / Partahi Lumbantoruan (34) / Daniel O'Neil (22) / Juan Ortiz (26) / Julia Pryde (23) / Waleed Shaalan (32) / Jamie Bishop (35) / Lauren McCain (20) / Michael Pohle Jr. (23) / Maxine Turner (22) / Nicole White (20) / Liviu Librescu (76) / Jocelyne Couture-Nowak (49) / Ross Alameddine (20) / Austin Cloyd (18) / Daniel Perez Cueva (21) / Caitlin Hammaren (19) / Rachael Hill (18) / Matthew La Porte (20) / Henry Lee (20) / Erin Peterson (18) / Mary Karen Read (19) / Reema Samaha (18) / Leslie Sherman (20) / Kevin Granata (45) / Committed suicide by shooting himself the same day and the wounded. [Hostages released] Didn't make the list (Murderpedia) and Shot dead by police at 4:48 p.m. ET after the hostages made a run for freedom (Wikipedia) and the wounded. Michael Grant Cahill, 62 / Libardo Eduardo Caraveo, 52 / Justin Michael DeCrow, 32 / John

P. Gaffaney, 56 / Frederick Greene, 29 / Jason Dean Hunt, 22 / Amy Sue Krueger, 29 / Aaron Thomas Nemelka, 19 / Michael S. Pearson, 22 / Russell Gilbert Seager, 51 / Francheska Velez, 21 / Juanita L. Warman, 55 / Kham See Xiong, 23 / Sentenced to death and the wounded. Parveen Ali (26) / Almir Olimpio Alves (43) / Marc Henry Bernard (44) / Maria Sonia Bernard (46) / Li Guo (47) / Lan Ho (39) / Layla Khalil (53) / Roberta King (72) / Jiang Ling (22) / Hong Xiu "Amy" Mao Marsland (35) / Dolores Yigal (53) / Hai Hong Zhong (54) / Maria Zobniw (60) / Committed suicide by shooting himself the same day and the wounded. Tshering Rinzing Bhutia (age 38), Doris Chibuko (age 40), Sonam Chodon (age 33), Grace Eunhae Kim (age 23), Katleen Ping (age 24), Judith Seymour (age 53), Lydia Sim (age 21), Didn't make the list (Murderpedia), Declared unfit to stand trial, "We did it again" ("That Other School Shooting," Jay Caspian Kang, *NY Times Magazine*) and the wounded.

Christoph K. Goertz, professor / Dwight R. Nicholson, chairman / Robert Alan Smith, assistant professor / Linhua Shan, a fellow graduate student / T. Anne Cleary, the assistant vice president for academic affairs / Committed suicide by shooting himself the same day and the wounded.

Anastasia Rebecca de Sousa and Committed suicide by shooting himself in the head the same day and the wounded. Ñacuñán Sáez, 37 (professor) and Galen Gibson, 18 (student) and Sentenced to two life sentences without the possibility of parole and the wounded. Norman Wallace and Sentenced to life imprisonment without parole and the wounded. Charged with two counts of attempted murder and the wounded.

10. [who survive] blood on my troubling hands leave me dry

— Ching-In Chen

50 Bullets, One Dead, and Many Questions

Teach that the alphabet begins with *n*.
Ask the question: how many bullets does it take?

Remember every bullet is a hymn
every hymn a taut line of rope
a row in a cotton field
a path to the back of the bus
a razor's edge as it cuts.

There are other ways.
Before the bullet there was the whip.
Before the whip there was the fist.
Take a wooden stick. Insert it with force
inside the rectum.
Name it poetry. Don't call it blood.
Consider it pomegranate stain, hibiscus leaf
your mama's lipstick, a cherry
lollipop, fire hydrant red.

Then

promote the word *peace,* and
see how their men are pieced together
like wood rot.

Put one of them in high office.
Tell the press we have gone post-black.

Whisper their names:

> Sean Bell
> Abner Louima
> Amadou Diallo
> Rodney King
> James Byrd
> Emmett Till
> ....
> ....
> ....
> ....
> ....

Fill in the blanks.

Remember the alphabet always begins with *n*.
Swallow. Regurgitate. Spit out.

Say it: *n*
Say it: *n-i*
Say it: *n-i-g*
Say it: *n-i-g-g*
Say it: *n-i-g-g-e*

Repeat after me: *n-i-g-g-e-r*

Whisper their names:

> Robbie Tolan
> Oscar Grant
> ....
> ....
> ....

Listen.

Skin as shattered glass.
Sound of rain on a tin roof.

Butterfly or bird
perched on wire.

Never mistake their winged song for spring.
They are watchers of the dead.

— Niki Herd

How to Not Get Killed by the NYPD

When you see the pitch-perfect black 4-door shaded windows roll
up on you, don't grip your wheel. Casually look over your shoulder
as a shaded window slips down. Don't think drive-by. Don't remember
history. It's only the police. Keep your hands on the wheel. In plain
view. It's the police. Keep your hands on the wheel. The light will turn
in your favor. Don't drive off. Keep your hands on the wheel. Wait,
with your left foot pressed hard on the clutch, right foot pressed lightly
on the brake. Hands on the wheel. Raise an eyebrow when the police
officer raises a question: what's the speed limit in New York City? Note:
the correct answer is 30, no matter the street, no matter the avenue,
no matter the faster moving highway traffic, the answer is 30   30.
Don't ask him to clarify. Don't smile. You are anxious. You will smile.
Don't explain when asked why you're smiling. Don't explain
your explanation when asked why you're explaining. Don't say:
we're blocking the road. Don't say: we're triple-parked.
Don't ask them to clarify the infraction. You are the infraction.
Don't remove your hands from the wheel. Accept
that you were pulled over. Accept the fact of the two fingers patting
the badge. Accept the hostile forehead, the condescension of the mouth.
Accept the fact of the wheel, troubling your hands. Accept their power.
>   Nod
when they repeat: we could give you a summons. Over & over & over
they will repeat this. Summons. Summons. Summons. We could
>   give you—.
The light will turn yellow. Red. Don't read the lights as a sign. The light
will turn green again. Don't let them see your jaw set in irritation. Accept
their power. Don't remember the history of police brutality in
>   New York. Keep
your hands in plain view. They shoot you in New York. 41 times.
4 times. In your grandmother's bathroom, they will shoot you. In front
of your house, they will call you burglar and shoot you. Don't remember
any of this. Don't ask them questions. Don't nod your head. Keep
>   your hands

on the wheel. Don't smile. Don't smile. Don't smile. Keep your hands
on the wheel. There is a right answer to their questions: yes, yes, yes, yes,
yes, yes, yes, you have the power, you have the power, you have the
       power, you
have—Keep your hands on the wheel. Drive off before they arrest you
for sitting too long at a green light. Avoid looking in your rearview
       mirror.
They will not drive off before you. They will haunt you in the daylight.
In their smoke-black 4-door (illegally) tinted windows, they mean
       to haunt.

— Metta Sáma

Baltimore 101

How are you afraid of a man
running away from you?
　　　　　—Toni Morrison

Fear is a magnetizer.
It changes the polarity of black bodies.
Makes them highly attractive to
bullets, police batons, Tasers,
white rage, white guilt,
and blue-eyed blondes.

Fear is a multiplier.
It turns children into men,
men and women into monsters,
and non-compliant teens
into dangerous gangs
and threatening mobs.

Fear is a magician.
It turns Hip Hop into gangster rap,
plastic toys into guns,
cigarillos, cellphones,
wallets, brazenness,
and extended index fingers
into high caliber weapons.

Fear is a revisionist history class.
It turns people of color into the
enslavers, confederate soldiers,
lynch mobs, klansmen, night riders
and terrorists.

Fear is a sniper.
It takes dead aim, aims to kill,
kills for sport and pleasure,
is pleased to take souvenirs,
and stuffs and mounts its trophies.

— Frank X Walker

Ghost Life

When my brother died we took turns
as ghosts in order to feel close to him.
It wasn't hard

to die all the time. We had experience
& all around us people we loved
slowly killed themselves

& buried each other. Why not bleed out
for a higher purpose than living.
From what we could tell, at least

memory, a lived thing, remained.
We could relive dap or a hug, just re-imagine
our brother with us. Our brother-

protector, brother-prankster, brother-priest.
We could confess anything to him & become
weightless, cast-off bodies until breath

returned to our sorrow-chafed throats.
We could even laugh sarcastically again
upon resurrection; the pain of return

worth the ghost life we knew would spit us out,
back into uniform violence & whatever between.
But we were his sisters. He wanted more than anger

for us. He could've let us look all the way through
that shoulder bullet hole, follow that fragment
into his heart, but he wanted us to see what we could do

when not pretending death felt better, eternally in media res,
wishing our brother, a god to us, stood watching over us
the way we imagined, almost alive.

— Khadijah Queen

Carcass

A body doesn't accuse you of things.
Silent. A body has a thug mouth,
huge gun. Or no gun. Or fists.
Or a wheelchair. Cane. Crutches.
A body doesn't fly. Limp. No muscle,
tongue. Hoodie, no handshake.
A body is drained. A body is prodded.
Mute strains of nothing. Broken.
Head twisted, shot, corroded, snapped.
A body doesn't rise. A body stays limp.
A body doesn't shake off pavement.
A body doesn't collide with stars.
A body's hours aren't hours,
they are centuries, redlined centuries.
A body can choke you. Break you.
Wreck you beyond reckoning.

— Allison Joseph

Hood HooDoo

These bodies lay down
Dragged pillar 2 post
Grieving dice rolling

The corner of church
Woman tears. We fly
Flags of threadbare

Black dresses. We carry
Book bags full of cop
Kill lesson

Plans.
My street smells like
Burning sage and wino breath.

The corner bodega has a sale on
Gilded coffins—
2 for one—

Secretly they take food stamps—
I burn like the imagined rubble
Of riot—The bootlegger has brewed

A concoction of fear and bravado
That I drink each time my child
Walks out the door.

— Danny Simmons

Elegy

I remember the boys & their open hands. High fives
    of farewell. I remember that the birches waved too,
        the white jagged limbs turning away from incessant wildfires.

The future wavered, unlike a question, unlike
    a hand or headstone. The future moved & the fields already knew it.

I remember the war of the alphabet, its ears sliced from its face.
    I know that
        language asks for blood.

The children of kudzu, lilac, the spit of unknown rivers. I remember
    the jury & the judge of
        the people. The buckshot that blew the morning's torso
            into smoke.

That last morning I begged the grandmothers to leave their rage
    next to red candles
        & worn photographs of their children & their blue-eyed
        grandson
            with a bleeding heart. The savior bled flowers.

I scattered the stones the trees bore. Gray vultures came for my children.
    They knew the old country better than me. They broke through
        skyscrapers & devoured both villain & hero.

& boys were pouring, wanted & unwanted & missing yet from the
    long mouth
        where their voices were forced to say they were nothing.
        But they were men,
                        invisible
        & native & guilty beyond their glottal doubt.

I remember calling out to the field where more boys knelt & swung
    through the air.
        I remember how their eyes rolled back in blood, milk,
            & gasoline. Their white teeth
                chewing cotton into shrouds, scars & sheets.

They gave me their last words, they gave me smiles for their fathers.
    They slept
        in my arms, dead & bruised. Long as brambles. The bullets
        in their heads
           & groins quieting like a day. The meat of nothing.

I held their million heads in my lap when the bodies were taken away.
    I don't know if what's left will dance or burn. I wash their eyelids
    with mint.

But let God beg pardon to them & their mothers.

& I don't know if the body is a pendulum of where love cannot go
    when the tongue is swollen with the milk of black boys.
        I pulled their lives from the trees & lawns & schools.
           The unlit houses & the river. Their forewings wet with
           clouds

& screaming. I won't leave them,

    huddled like bulls inside the stall of a word. I am the shriek,
    the suture, the rose

        petal shook loose from their silence.

— Rachel Eliza Griffiths

mothers

become shroud dirty rags of a holy book that supposedly forgot
to stand vigil over our children ransomed to sun beneath each
month's moon hidden or full the daughters of other mothers
themselves likely near death send us prayer shawls send us poems
send us slabs of crystals a mother opens her mouth it is always
wailing blood metallic bullets ride the mucous in her throat tease
the pregnant ball of fire brewing inside her head we open our
mouths to allow the blood to speak through light that does not
choke the blood speaks through light that out races breath mothers
swallow all the blood their stomachs can hold licking sidewalks
playground swings back seats of dirty cop cars we become vampires
who have no fear of light who have no fear of sexy silver bullets
trying to crawl up our thighs we no longer fear the photographs
of our children dying with mouths wide open their last sentences
holographic prayers caught in between flash and light we sprout
swords smiles that curse the memory that your first word was *light*
is the balm traveling quieting a hysterical womb your first word
was *light* now you swim with dolphins feeding them tiny particles
of light filament your small teeth would chew and chew all the light
your mouth could hold you later fed the ice to your baby brother
calling crushed ice *stars for a baby brother* it has been a year full
of a thousand years each month each day chasing the other inside
my womb pulling grasping cramping for a blood birth of history
herstory already told already buried already rotten a year full of limp
apology dead proclamation faceless monsters breaking the shadow
dance of other children more mothers drink the blood appear in
daylight wild eyes speaking searing truths our daughters hold so
much of the mothers grief inside their own wombs that become
tombs for babies that scream *no i'm not coming to this world* this
plight this revolution that is brewing inside a vampire's apron
pockets inside grandmother's kitchens where they are stitching
witching weaving brewing ancient fodder to feed another storm
of harnessed lynched shackled light mothers become a season unto

poems to stretch the sky

themselves storing winter blood mothers have become too familiar with death as personal as the found wisps of a son's single strand of hair or the stale perfume stained handkerchief folded hidden inside your child's pocket we are reminded in between each touch of warm lavender jasmine lemon cypress water cleaning stroking kissing soothing the cavity created by nine sexy silver bullets that we are mothers swimming strong in rivers so ancient they need no names in between the honey and rosemary balm massage in between each finger each toe we are reminded that we have always buried our dead and we have always raised our dead we are ancient vampires reckless eating stars lights full moons sexy silver bullets blue monsters we are strange language strange face strange dance we are the ghosts of all the children speaking through the smoke.

— Jaki Shelton Green

Da da di da

these white, shroud-bound bodies:
once sun-brown children with wild hair,
coin-eyes that glittered in buzzing luster,
fireflies in dust skies,
zephyr wind tender
scented in jasmine and honey.

these bodies wrapped in gauze,
split open just hours ago,
someone's meat to mangle
with tester bullets and bombs, the kind meant
to warn (non) citizens to run
animals in shoes
when between the sea and dust:
      the protestor and the riot gear,
          home and the corner store
a stone's throw skipping,
a lullaby swaying from mother-lips,
call to

                            a child could cross
that in sound

they were just feeding the chickens
corn from lined palms,
rippling mutilation in the grooves.
      they were just playing
      in a playground
          walking down the street
             being other   black

what is the song
children sing when dreaming
listless? does it sound like this?

— Raina J. León

WORDS

for Amadou Diallo

Forty-one bullets –
nineteen in the soft plaster
of his body.
The ritual marks
link the cracked wall,
the bloody palm-print;
the heavy meat
of his heart,
cooled.

Blood flooded his lungs
their sea
of cilia, air and water
rose to his eyes.

His flesh –
the blue bitter night.

All manner of speaking fails.
The sounds of guns are near.

I would run though this city shouting
beware, beware but I'd be telling a truth
we already know.

Tell me: Did he speak in his own tongue at the end?
Implore the stunned stars,
utter the unutterable name,
fire his whole life into a single,
final, vowel?

— Veronica Golos

Emmett Till's name still catches in my throat

like syllables waylaid in a stutterer's mouth.
A fourteen-year-old stutterer, in the South
to visit relatives and to be taught
the family's ways. His mother had finally bought
that White Sox cap; she'd made him swear an oath
to be careful around white folks. She'd told him the truth
of many a Mississippi anecdote:
Some white folks have blind souls. In his suitcase
she'd packed dungarees, T-shirts, underwear,
and comic books. She'd given him a note
for the conductor, waved to his chubby face,
wondered if he'd remember to brush his hair.
Her only child. A body left to bloat.

— Marilyn Nelson

The sight of his fist is fatal

for Michael Brown

Skip humanity. Hold them to the superhuman
and the conventions don't apply.

How many times will smoke rise over a city,
over every city, every night?

I felt like a five-year-old holding onto Hulk Hogan.
Holding onto a what?

Don't burn anything. Stay calm, again.
Justice promises to come from the future.

Laws promise to become better laws.
The price of time travel is coming down.

Heartbreak breaks the heart
and leaves everything else intact.

How small I felt.
Like a demon, that's how angry he looked.

Hard facts. Yellow socks disappear and appear,
glass flies through the air.

Justifiable. We have so many ugly words
for murder.

— Kenji C. Liu

Word of the Day

My little blond, blue-eyed neighbor loves

    his word of the day.

I have given him *vestibule, watermelon tourmaline,*

    perambulate, canine, harmonious

I have not offered

    taser, intimidation, racial profiling,

      rough ride (new to my vocabulary as well).

He will learn those words, those phrases soon enough

    (though, most likely, not by experience).

I hope he will come to understand that being ignorant

    is never a solution.

I hope he will come to use those words well

    by raising his voice.

— Marilyn Singer

The Definition of Privilege

after Michael Cirelli

Nathan and Davis had the wad of bills we stole from Davis'
father's work coat so when they led us down the block to *Hop In*
we followed because we were thirsty and had no idea the darker
skinned of us would only minutes later end up with their chests on
the pavement, a stranger's hands scaling their waistlines and thighs
while the lighter skinned of us would watch from the sidewalk with
our tongues pretzeled into knots like the barrels of cartoon rifles
and I was nine-years-old on the verge of a fifteen-year obsession
to prove I was not whatever it was that kept me off the pavement
alongside Nathan and Davis, first by quitting classical piano lessons
and growing my hair out and studying the blues then traveling
across continents with groups of quasi-guilty Christians to build
schools in Peru or community centers in Israel or soccer fields in
Mexico or Whereverthefuck and then working up the nerve to
rock matching track suits every day in the upper lot at *Pioneer High
School* and basketball jerseys two sizes too-big and start drinking
forties of Old English malt liquor like Ice Cube with kids who lived
in Eagle Point and North Maple and reciting Too Short verses to my
crush at the bus stop where I eventually started smoking so much
weed before school that I got suspended for vomiting in the trash
can during my third period English class and had to go to summer
school which I really used as an opportunity to distribute the first
of many mixtapes in my very serious rap career that I swore would
be my "ticket outta here" on which I used spoonfuls of words my
mother didn't understand until I finally (not somehow) landed in
college and registered mostly for classes in which I was the only
white person where a professor asked me to share the earliest
memory I had of race so I told the story of Nathan and Davis and
Hop In and the stranger's hands and she asked why whiteness made
me so uncomfortable and I said *It doesn't* but then I said *Because I
don't ever think about it* and she replied *Not having to think about*

something sounds like a pretty amazing privilege and then I started seeing kids who looked just like me (everywhere) whose whole lives were bending into knots like the barrels of cartoon rifles just to prove they weren't whatever it was that kept me off the pavement when I was nine-years-old, which is to say guilty for something they didn't do which is to say *I never owned slaves, I'd never say the N-word—ever—*which is to say invisible which is to say *I don't really have a race* which is to say the option of silence.

— Adam Falkner

Drive-by

*Bah daaaaaah! Bah daaaaaah! Bah doo dah! Dah dah daaaah dee
daaaaaah! Bah daaaaaah!*

Must be the dread-
       locks, no, the red-hot SUV, no
the deer-in-headlights glare after
       a rear-end accident, the shock
of the hit-&-run, the latest irony of my existence
       since my brachial plexus snapped
& left me a palsied leper.

*Bah daaaaaah! Bah daaaaaah! Bah doo dah! Dah dah daaaah dee
daaaaaah! Bah daaaaaah!*

Must be that I am too
       helpful to Miss Gold-Star Gumshoe.
Must be hiding something be-
       hind my eagerness to hand over Florida
registration & grinning license pic,
       riding through this side of Milwaukee's worst
at 2 a.m. *I had a gig on*

32nd & Burleigh, I muster,
       pointing to a beat-up trumpet case, but
Jazz? Cannot be that simple.
       We just need to take you in to check things out.
I remain silent.
*Bah daaaaaah! Bah daaaaaah! Bah doo dah! Dah dah
daaaah dee daaaaaah! Bah daaaaaah!*
       wailing inside on the ride to the precinct, where

Turn! Flash *Turn!*
    Flash *Turn!* Flash
welcomes me. Steeled into submission, I
    sleep. Four hours pass. I awake, railing
Why am I still here? Why am I still
    here? Why ... Reluctantly, I
am released.

Bah daaaaaah! Bah daaaaaah! Bah doo dah! Dah dah daaaah dee
daaaaaah! Bah daaaaaah!

Now, I seethe every drive-by, your
    public service announcement, the roar
of your sirens. The red, white & blue, flashing, threatens
    my sable soul, today, on this mountain. I want to die, no,
kill a little more each time you hover,
    searching for the next one of us to put away.

Bah daaaaaah! Bah daaaaaah! Bah doo dah! Dah dah daaaah dee daaaaaah!
Bah daaaaaah

— L. Lamar Wilson

Decoded

You / I
   take / nurture
      my / your
         bag / blood
           and / and
              pour / fill
                its / your
                  t / emptiness
                      on / from
                        the / the
                      sidewalk / sky

If / When
  I / I
 wear / undress
    my / your
      hoodie / skin
        it / it
      is not / is
         in / from
        danger / safety
         it / it
        is not / is
         in / from
        solidarity / alienation
          it / it
          is / is not
        showmanship / reality

The / A
Interviewer / God
    asked / answered
      if / when
        I / I
        studied / neglected
          how / why
        Buddy Holly / Little Richard
          disarmed / provoked
            all / one
              black / white
              audiences / emptiness

My / Your
primary / final
    album / silence
      in / on
      middle / infinite
        school / repeat
        was / is
          Warren G's / Kenny G's
          Regulators / lawlessness

"If / When
    I / you
    had / lose
      a / the
        son / moon
        he'd / it
          look / blinds
            like / unlike
          Trayvon" / anything

Our / Your
children / ancestors
will / won't
be / be
responsible / forgiven
for / despite
the / any
debts / surplus
we / you
have not / have
paid / assumed
in / from
blood / myths

The / A
white / black
girl / boy
on / in
stage / reality
said / listened
she / he
prayed / knew
Trayvon / Trayvon
reached / left
for / despite
the / a
gun / prayer

— Jon Sands

Future Crimes

if a man is constantly guilty
for what goes on in his mind
give me the electric chair
for all my future crimes ....
                              — Prince

I am guilty.
I am cop guilty.
I am MERCEDES guilty.
I am shoot you in the back guilty .
I know I am guilty
For what goes on in my mind.
I know I am guilty
When the cop pulls me over.
I know he knows I am guilty.
So these bullets in my back
As I try running,
So this lead tattoo
Against my shirt:
I had this coming.
I took a ride, love.
This crime of passion
That sets me free,
That sets me free,
I am constantly guilty
For what goes on in his mind,
The mind of this cop,
Who knows if he doesn't stop me now,
My loose black body in the world...
I know who you are, says the cop,
And it's not mistaken identity,
Because we know I am guilty
For all my future crimes,

poems to stretch the sky

For all my future crimes.
This is me, chosen, turning on
My heels,
My weird, half broken gallop,
Wishing for wings, wishing for lift
Wishing for luck, wishing for bad aim, or
A shell, spent just before the target is kissed.
This is me, selected, my black back running
Out of the life I thought I had,
Out of the simple boredom of the day.
Sooner or later, my breathing kin,
This is what goes on in our minds.

for Walter Scott

— Cornelius Eady

Every 28 Hours

Every 28 hours, I find myself wanting to pray.

Every 28 hours, I hear the constant clap getting closer.

Every 28 hours, I wonder if my phone may ring.
　　　　Will it be my eclipsed brother's breath?
　　　　Or my sisters, nephews, nieces, the list
　　　　includes all of us.

Every 28 hours, a black body drops like roadkill
　　　　and that is worth less than abandoned storefronts
　　　　or a broken window.

Every 28 hours, a student I may have fed with food
　　　　cooked in my own kitchen may disappear.

Every 28 hours, the jangling of a mother's jagged
　　　　tears drags along eardrums.

Every 28 hours, you will hear someone say
　　　　he got what he deserved and why
　　　　are they so destructive?

Every 28 hours, an officer's aim is rewarded with pay,
　　　　vacation, and benefits, including breath.

Every 28 hours, a parent wonders if the child
　　　　they carried will be discarded, a case dismissed.

Every 28 hours, a death is backed up with armored
　　　　vehicles, automatic weapons, teargas, bulletproof
　　　　vests and shields. We are not in a distant war.

Every 28 hours, we are still counting, shaking,
        sweating, breathing, unless we reach our 28th hour.

We are at home—so they say, for every hour.

Written for a post-Ferguson protest at Binghamton City Hall –
Binghamton, NY November 25, 2014

— Tara Betts

Anti Elegy

The faces of our death are unresolved. The body, identified, is
    confirmed by music. Rag time. Big band blood. We all look alike.
      We're prayers. The coroner's baby grand piano
        in a cold drawing room.

We were not identified by our teeth [broken] or by our country [broken].
    These are the words we will not be.
      Will you finish this poem or give the back of its mouth to
      the gun?

The hearts, terra cotta blue, were buried beneath birch.
    Drop bread from the hands that push sentences into our cages.
      Murder the grooms
        & Apollos. Drag your chariots over the head of Orpheus
          where a headless agony rolls like a kickball
            in a Jasper road.

The business of caretakers? Bet on that
    staying platinum. The more black you buy & bury
      the harder heaven shines its pennies.

Bless this nation of uncertain chambers. Bludgeon the orchestra with
    blues. Plastic bags
      of glory going for a name on any corner
        where a pick-up game distracts the night from the black
        bruise
          swinging in the jaundice of a streetlight.

The metaphors grieve their own offspring. The riddles are tired of
    numbers & bony ghettos.
      The scandal of marrow as it witnesses our gaze.
      The crap game of bones in repose.

— Rachel Eliza Griffiths

The Talk

　　　　When two people love each other
or think they love each other
or think they see love in someone
else　they will try to be alone
together　which is better then being alone
by yourself　unless you loan your self out to others
in which you might not get your self
back　　so
　　　　when you find someone of interest
show interest in getting closer
while cautious not to come off too strong
or too easy so　give them space
keep your eyes down in fact
just cross to the other side of the street
people may see you as threat or suspect and
　　　　when they see you as a suspect
keep your eyes down put your hands
up say yes sir and no sir and I'm going
to reach into my pocket and take out
my I.D. sir and no sir I do not have a weapon
cause you are a weapon your mind and body and
breath are a weapon
and like any weapon you are a piece of art
and like any art they'll want to lock you up
behind glass and look at you and never
ever touch you and all you want to be
all we all want to be is touched　　　　so
　　　　when you find someone you want
to touch and who'll want to touch you back
make sure you hear words like honey
and sweetie and pumpkin pie and
beau but not so much
that you don't hear them from anyone
special　and not so much that you don't believe them

when heard and not so much that they turn
into words like jezebel and black
bastard and fucking
faggot and goddamn
dyke because these words will come
at night when you are walking alone
on the street grab at your breath take you
from your body and rip away your mind and you are mine
my child or worse still
when you find someone willing
to have a child with you and with you
alone you will know
the cacophony of a clock ticking past
curfew you will know the cold sweat
of an insomnia sheet you will know
the world is your partner limbs over yours
lips to your ear
saying *I will be here*
tomorrow and tomorrow I will
kill everyone you love.

— Quincy Scott Jones

Buck.

seems some want
      some body bodied
   on some sweet street meat.

        come and go get it!
         we won't scuffle
but you want us to, too. tool
cocked back to make a no way way
you let yourself in
us. umber-husked,
such a dirty look
   is a dirty talk
begging for the something long
in your dom palm
what smokes after doing it.

you make us scream the shut up.

you ever never hankered for surrender,
so the hard way: cuff some or stick it.
such a hurry! look
       don't sweat,   don't fret.
you've ever done this before—just fudge we're not real,
        too dark to
tell.
     let's role:

we were fondling for your piece and finger banging a cashbox peeped
through convenient ballistic glass and face down assed-out lawned
till we popped the juice came out us once our middle finger resisted
lunged shiv-ish fit to shoot shot while the woofers woofed their stiff
trap beats, you said. and:

wanted us in the buck
                    so buck us some
                we'll buck up after by candlelight, petal arrangements,
and we shall, we shall
                 like fucking champs, we; and you're some machine
ain't you
all up in it, so we gotta be down,
    up to here.

— Douglas Kearney

Duck Season/Rabbit Season

Sometimes the exotic can be right in front of you.[1]
— Kehinde Wiley

In this photograph you are lion-like, toothless, fraudulent.[2]
— *Uniglory*, Jen Hofer

wide ranging large carnivores like this bear are particularly
vulnerable to becoming road kill.[3]
— Wikipedia

"knock on wood I've never seen a Game Warden"
— Anonymous Exotic Animal Dealer

Di a ontiman si a tigri, a lon teki en gon, dan a sutu a tigri kiri.

[1] like an ill manila ts'i'ii[mosquito] yellow jacket bumble taser justified pounce on the *not again*pleasantry of buffalo antelope & wildebeest no persecution plain clothed weave about chokeholds specter of an eye out of orbit the hand of father reaches towards the heavenly chaplain for a loosie the traffic of street sport makes Call of Duty a shielded hunger for warrants & arrests knock & announce *such a handsome wunderkind how you carry yourself how you exist Oakland panther Simba of Tulsa you yield my quota Mighty Joe Young* the livestock auction shuts down online the unbecoming conduct of a predator reflects onto the caricatured carriage homebound on platforms suspect zhinii[black] hide is by birth concealed arsenal often claret dusted sclera admits *too much umber must never be mistaken for Bambi*

When the hunter saw the jaguar,
he ran for his gun and shot the jaguar dead.

[2] jurisdiction on the isle of malign w/ gendarmerie blue offers a weekend getaway far beyond ranches in Texas or cells on Rikers *you my dearest gravy Zebra irresistible European badger no hostile Congolese honey fallen on enforced sword by the city of St. Louis Christ you are a remarkable creature aging poached rhino in a*

hoodie saintly you are bejeweled wallaby sometimes the gamers' caravan does not want the meat they prefer to mount the head in mugshots *Oh if only I could stuff you*

Yu mus leri a pikin fu luku bun fosi a e koti strati abra.

[3] in passage just a minor cabin incursion hazard just easier to separate the head pummel a fist into a feminine version nihimá[our] [mother] *becomes blue-tugee island make way for stray puppies to clean the ground insatiable mutts drink a cruor that is opulent & profound they understand little difference between yours & a brush tail possum* arresting brown boy laying in the unsullied cutgrass *comply or canoodle pavement*

You need to teach the child to look carefully
before crossing the street.

— LaTasha N. Nevada Diggs

[1] The poem contains phrases written in Sranan Tongo, a creole language from Suriname and Diné (Navaho).

Always in Season

It doesn't shock me anymore
A black man shot
While handcuffed on his stomach
In a train station
Or a black boy shot
Walking to his father's house
With a bag of Skittles
Or a black teen shot
For playing his music
Too loud
Or while on his knees
Asking for help after
Surviving a car crash

I was fifteen when I was told
All I had to do was make it
To twenty-five
Survival rates go up then
Made me wonder if
Blue whales and bald eagles
Knew how long they had to live
To make it over the hump
Surely I've stolen home by now
A year older than the jersey number
Jackie Robinson wore in Brooklyn
A mere seven years from double dodging
My life expectancy

But today I read about
Garrick and Carl Hopkins
Sixty and sixty-one
Brothers who bought a piece of land
In the hills of West Virginia

And the white man who lived next door
Who shot them dead like deer
While they walked round their tool shed
Where he felt they had no right to be walking
Flashback 2008 in the hood barbershop
Where targets of all ages gather to laugh
Tell lies and signify
"What y'all think it's gon mean, having a black president?"
"Ain't gon mean shit bruh. Ain't gon change a got damn thing."

— Howard L. Craft

Static, After Getting Stopped by the Cops While Flying to Stop Another Metahuman Because, Well, We All Know Why Any Black Superhero Would Get Stopped by the Cops

It wasn't so much / the unwarranted frisk / that pissed me off. / Wasn't the bullshit that I / "fit the description" / because I ain't never seen / no description / that includes / last seen flying / on a metal saucer / propelled by electromagnetic force. // It wasn't even that they stopped me. / In Dakota / that's inevitable / as death / or taxes / or death / at the hands / of some trigger-happy cops — / it wasn't that I was scared / to die. / I could've disarmed them, / easy. // It was that even as Static / I could be stopped — / and not by someone like me, / someone with powers, / but someone with just the power / of a badge / and a gun / and the idea that made him / stronger than me. // It was that somewhere / someone like me / needed to be stopped / and wasn't / because two men / were too preoccupied / with stopping me. // It was that even with all my powers / I was powerless.

— Malcolm Friend

Static's Elegy for Black Bodies

Because it could have been me seems too easy. Because it couldn't have been me, right? Because I save lives every day. Because I stop the bad guys. Because I have superpowers—and not just the ones I use to fight crime but others, too, like posing for pictures next to politicians and getting the key to the city, like my music never too loud, like I never look suspicious, like my mask less threatening than a hoodie.

Because I'm tired of saving lives just to watch my people lose theirs. Because the night sky seems darker with every Black soul that reaches heaven. Because what kind of superhero are you if you can't protect your own? Because every time a cop arrives after one of my fights I'm afraid they'll mistake me for the bad guy. Because every time a cop arrives after one of my fights I'm afraid they'll know I'm not the bad guy but the outcome will be the same.

Because I'm not a superhero, not when I take off my mask. When it's gone, I'm Virgil. Which is to say I'm nameless. Which is to say it could have been me.

— Malcolm Friend

The Emperor's Deer

I.

Their noises make you think
they are crying or suffering.
They have learned to bow.
Even the fawns bow, centuries
of bowing
in their blood.

They are not considered wild.
Precious pests litter parks
with dung, take over the roads.
Sweet nuisance worth
saving, thinning these herds
is a last resort—once
a capital offense to spill
their endangered blood.

They are so used to humans, it is scary.

II.

Our cries are heard as noise,
our suffering considered
natural. Native citizens,
we are not free
to roam or deemed sacred
like Japanese bowing deer protected
as messengers of the gods.

Nara, Japan is known for its temples,
shrines to peace.
America is known for its churches,
segregated Sundays.

This is not Nara, Japan.
Hunted, it is always
open season. The sight
of dark skin brings out the wild
in certain human breeds.
Bowing, hands up
or any other gesture of surrender
makes no difference.

They slay our young and leave them
in the streets, expect us to walk away
and wonder, after centuries
why we are not used to this—

grieving masses treated
like waste, filthy herds
thinned at will.

III.

To be clear, this is America
and we are not deer
We are not deer
We are not dear
Here

— Kamilah Aisha Moon

thriller

the time i hit a deer on the ohio turnpike
outside cleveland and a police officer

arrived quicker than a meal at a well run cafe.
and there was the time an officer stopped me when

my car broke down and he was off duty and out
with his lady and he still stopped and gave me

some flares. still, when the police stop me now
all i see is vincent price in one of his movies.

ghoulish face, 'dr phibes,' perhaps, something
shocking about to happen. i am more uneasy

than a child lost in a supermarket. this is not a
movie. this is real and long lasting like years ago

angry officers pulled us over in the dark of night
on sargent road, hyattsville, maryland, cocked

their 12 gauges at us as if we are targets in a
carnival game, flipped the n-word naturally;

it flowed from their mouths like hoots from owls,
squawks of seagulls. they dared us to dash. we didn't

oblige, we let vince have his fun, put us in his
movie; i hear the laugh from 'thriller' every time.

michael jackson is alive but has not yet sung his
song. so it is just vincent price, his badge,

Resisting Arrest

gun, the sick sound of something sinister, forever
planted in my mind like finger writing in concrete,

nothing yet has been able to erase that night because
too many of us have been in these movies and sometimes

you get cast again, and sometimes you get cast again, and
sometimes...

— Brian Gilmore

In America's Mirror

Neither bridge nor trapeze.
Neither absence nor plot.

Just a hobo with a scent of the scavenger,
the romanticized stink of a jackal

in Darfour, Port-au-Prince, or Mexico City—

(bullet-riddled skull there,
neat cough,
helix, calcium)—

but neither tundra nor cobblestone.

Neither sharecropper nor fireworks nor pillar—
                    just a callous brunette
                    gerrymandering the night.

Flotsam. Labyrinth.
Unkempt ambition.
Ashes for a shallow urn.

A little too dangerous,
a little thistle.

All longitude. All moonshine.

But neither smoke nor spinet, neither blue-
stem nor stammer in the white mayhem.

— Lynne Thompson

Campaign Speech, 1896:
"The Scourge of Foreign Elements"

The civilizing effects of modernity
have not yet smoothed the rough edges
of rummies, watch-stuffers, prostitutes
or thimble-riggers. Those who inflate
prices, tip scales, extort or confuse,
bring decay and imbecility, scandal and reproach.
We can no longer tolerate barefaced jobbery.
Citizens, lend your indignation to the cause.
The civilizing effects of modernity
demand the placement of public interests
where they properly belong, in the ameliorating
hands of authority. When vigilance
against sharks is allowed to weaken,
the poor are exposed in a forlorn, helpless
condition. Agents of bawdy-houses and thieves
make their harvest on the hapless,
who are strangers to our moral crusade
and the civilizing effects of modernity.

— Kim Roberts

"Maroon" Equasions: 2015

What would slave-rebels make of this world
we've inherited? What will our futures become?
When young militants, we fought gallantly
against repression and racist terror—Slavery
in another form. Africans stood up, faced klansmen
amidst our daughter's dynamited churches;
walked with the martyred remains of murdered
prophets—Malcolm, Martin, Medgar. All for
elusive gains: freedoms and documents created
while we were chained, sold on auction blocks.
Freedom and its fruits? Why we've never known it.
We Bantu people who move as pariahs in Anglo
Paradise, wearing bulls-eyes upon our dusky skins.
Of course, as human beings, whose Ancestors,
in the Nile and Tigris valleys, pioneered Civilization,
we recognize our duty to further democracy
and true human rights; however, now we'd just
settle for drug-free communities, and protection
from predators, who murder our people in
the thousands, garbed in fascist legions
of "squad car/crime-fighting" blue." Patrollers"
in 21st Century slavery, making sure that "Thugs"
won't challenge the Corporate Authority's rule.

"Maroons" were one of the names called slave-revolt guerillas
fighting against the "New World" plantations.
Nat Turner,Gullah Jack, Denmark Vesey, Gabriel and Nannie
Prosser, Harriet Tubman, Captain John Brown: 19th Century
freedom-fighters against U.S. Slavery.

"Patrollers" were the poor whites and their allies, who were hired
to " police" the "New World" plantations, with
the rights to capture and/or murder escaped slaves.

— Askia M. Toure'

Emancipation Thieves

My emancipation don't fit your equation
        — Lauryn Hill, "Lost Ones"

I.
When the deputies knock
@ our door, I rub my eyes,
listen to the charge in disbelief,
turn to my closet, trade
pajamas for suit, black hard bottoms,
wait for my hands to be cuffed
behind me, in front of my wife
& son, his cries chasing me
down the walkway. The deputies
lower my head, push me
into the press
of the cruiser's backseat. This
is mistaken identity, the eyes
of neighbors @ sunrise,
the long ride up Broadway
past the cleaners, the liquor
store, the drug store.
            An escort to stares,
questions, fingerprints,
simmering rage, the wife
that goes about her day,
gives a speech @ a luncheon
like I'm not locked up,
asks *Are you sure*
you didn't do anything?

These are the minutes
you won't forget, memories
that gnaw, lash. As trust
unravels, leaves you—beaten.

II.

How hard
must fists
be hurled
to bruise?
Brother endures
a windmill
of knuckle,
white & black: off-
duty   not
offering
protection. Hands
cuffed @ back,

)... waited for my hands to be cuffed
behind me, in front of my wife
& son, his cries...(

you cannot fight,
flesh a sponge,
soak of blows.
Another
& another
(jaw   breaks)
Another
& another
(eyes   seal)
Another
& an   other
& another
& an   other
&...

Son before my son, dark-
eyed echo of my birth,
I have failed you. Please
forgive the fall.

III.
Tell me—
truly—how
are we
still standing?

— Mitchell L.H. Douglas

RoboCop

a Larry Davis story

What is it like! We have a saying
around the precinct, you know.
*"Nineteen years in the South Bronx beat
hardens a man, even a Catholic priest."*
Don't write that...but it is pretty funny.

If you seen the things I've seen...
I don't drink before the job. It slows
down my reflexes and when you deal
with pieces of shit like Larry Davis,
you got to be ready. It's Kill or be Kill.
Is that fucking simple! These animals
don't care. They ready to eat his bones.

What do I Feel? I don't feel shit. I've been
desensitize to this shit hole since my rookie year.
The Mayor doesn't care. These Jew bastards
burn people out to collect the insurance money.

What's my stake? I live in fucking Staten Island.
You think I want to drive here to get kill.
Fuck you! We all toil in these sewers.
I just want to make it home every night.
I hate everything about this place. Why? 'cause
they don't appreciate the work that I do.

I haven't survived for 20 years because I care,
No! Whatever it takes man. Look at me!
Took a bullet to my knee, my hand, my thigh
I'm fucking RoboCop now, and for what?
So these animals can let him go free.
Let me tell you something, everyone!
And I mean—every-one wanted him dead.
No one—wanted the paper work.

— Ricardo Nazario y Colón

The Suits of Your Skins

for Ciara, David, and Perre

A simple grey suit behind glass.
I stood close enough to be breathless.
The shooter was almost this close
to Harvey Milk, a man he dropped.

Faded sepia stains the once
white shirt, surrounds bullet
holes that cling to frayed fabric.
There is more than one
hole. Black people know there
is always more than one hole.

There is more than one black
child standing beside me.
I hold my breath for three
inhales, three exhales for
each because their heads
come at the cheapest price.

And the whispers will say
they deserved restraints,
the beatings were expected,
they were due for death.

And what to tell the black girl
when the magazines erase her
one page at a time. She could
disappear and no one will put
her lost body in a headline.
Her limbs anathema to the news.

And what to tell the two queer
black boys who could be my sons,
who could be beaten into misshapen
blood melons and left like loosely-tied
garbage bags. What to tell the black
children who would be told to never
reach for anything—not a cell phone,
a wallet, a bb gun, a water pistol,
a dashboard, a doorknob, rights.

And what to tell the white classmates
who do not understand experiments
are carried out on outcasts first. (Say *stop*
because you do not want to say *I am next*.)

And what to tell all the students when
assault vehicles click out of stockpiles
and occupy the streets with tear gas.

Yes, I am looking at a jacket, pants, and shirt
wrinkled after a long day at work, then death.
This suit of a dead white gay man on a stamp
and immortalized in film. The three huddled
around me mean more than a suit for a man
that people still pity. I look still as I tremble
inside for the three students around me—
each of them a brilliant burst just opening
that could be extinguished and only folks
like me will canonize them. I echo my loves.

I write you down, sketch your stamps,
remember your jokes, insist the suits
of your skins are not for idle display.

— Tara Betts

The Gun Joke

It's funny, she says, how many people are shocked
by this shooting and the next and next and the next.
She doesn't mean funny as in funny, but funny
as in blood soup tastes funny when you stir in soil.
Stop me if you haven't heard this one:
A young man/old man/teenage boy walks into
an office/theater/daycare/club and empties
a magazine into a crowd of strangers/family/students.
Ever hear the one about the shotgun? What do you call it
when a shotgun tests a liquor store's bulletproof glass?
What's the difference between a teenager
with hands in the air and a paper target charging at a cop?
What do you call it when a man sets his own house on fire,
takes up a sniper position, and waits for firefighters?
Stop me if you haven't heard this one:
The first man to pull a gun on me said it was only a joke,
but never so much as smiled. The second said
this is definitely not a joke, and then his laughter crackled
through me like electrostatic—funny how that works.
When she says it's funny she means funny
as in crazy and crazy as in this shouldn't happen.
This shouldn't happen as in something is off. Funny as in
off—as in, ever since a small caliber bullet chipped his spine,
your small friend walks kinda funny and his smile is off.

— Jamaal May

To Freddie Gray on the Occasion of your Death at the Hands of Peace Officers

Peace and violence cannot occupy the same space at the same time

Your eyes gaze on a face.
by years of squeezed air in lungs.

A signal sparked by-passing a "Go Slow" cautioned
by years of squeezed air in lungs often malfunctioned.

The pipe ever near now pocketed.
You cannot do two things at the same time; run fast,

breathe, breathe, while trying to dig inside a pocket
that hides the contents asthmatics require: you fall,

collapsed the effort to breathe,
choking, gasping , no air. Hands cuff your wrists.

Pulled up short,
your legs refuse your weight. You sag.

Hands pull. You swoon. Hands lift you and slam the floor
with your body. Your hands claw at your pocket, limited range

no breath. You cannot breathe.
Your chest heaves, billows fail to exhale: A sharp right, then a left

then shock of "Wham"
your head against metal walls. There is no breath left in you.

All the years left unlived
fly past the doors; moving, moving. A shaft of light,

a new voice, as you float inside a breathless van.
No one comes when you call. Your mother is working. Your father says,

"Be a man. Stop crying like a baby.
Big boys don't cry." And so you don't and tears mix with blood

congealed mucus the dying release
upon death's contact so now at peace, you arrive at this place

by hands of Peace Officers who offer
a swift ride without seat belts, without restraints, the violence of
        not caring,

contradicts the presence of anger, of fear
and the refusal to accept the consequences of their actions; all plea,

"Innocent" and "Not guilty"
of being negligent of knowing you were slipping in the unrestrained
        space

provided for by an unintentional ride.
No flowers or songs; no marching or petitions can reverse your status.

Punishment comes. Time sorts out details, suggesting
it all happened eons ago when conscious decisions were made.

This side for you. That side reserved for those whose fathers own the
        vehicles,
the uniforms, guns and all the men who load bullets, line streets
        and carry batons.

To them is the victory and spoils.
To you an early grave, ready or not; you are dead. Your pipe

will never pump into your mouth
nor will your clogged bronchial struggle to expand to suck in air.

You have no need for that now. But when you can,
come gently into young dreams. Tell the young men: "Live! Live!"

Twenty-five is too soon to die unfulfilled.
Hope is redemption of violence seeking to displace peace.

— Rashidah Ismaili

The Ninth of August, 2014*

after Mike Brown who had his hands up and didn't even know it

It could have been early morning Principe Hill
in Spain, but was afternoon just north of St. Louis,
instead. At your feet lay Shawn Bell, Oscar Grant,
Eric Gardner and to your right the faces
of my nephew, my brother, my unborn son.

The light must have blindfolded your eyes
and you couldn't see any faces, only the barrel
of a .40 caliber gun glinting in Missouri sun.
Their uniforms are always a variation of the same.

And maybe, just maybe, your back against America,
you realized that no amount of bullets could hurt
you anymore, your only regret that no one
stepped forward to offer you a Cigarillo
or was allowed to kneel over your body to pray.

*Based on Francisco Goya's painting, *The Third of May, 1808.*

— James E Cherry

Imagine

after the news of the dead whether or not we
knew them we are saying thank you
            — W. S. Merwin

A blanket of fresh snow
makes any neighborhood idyllic.
Dearborn Heights indistinguishable from Baldwin Hills,
South Central even—
until a thawing happens and residents emerge
into the light. But it almost never snows in L.A.,
and snows often in this part of Michigan—
a declining wonderland, a place not to stand out
or be stranded like Renisha was.

Imagine a blonde daughter with a busted car
in a suburb where a brown homeowner
(not taking any chances)
blasts through a locked door first,
checks things out after—
around the clock coverage and the country beside itself
instead of the way it is now,
so quiet like a snowy night
and only the grief of a brown family (again)
around the Christmas tree, recalling
memories of Renisha playing
on the front porch, or catching flakes
as they fall and disappear
on her tongue.

They are left to imagine
what her life might have been.
We are left to imagine the day
it won't require imagination
to care about all of the others.

— Kamilah Aisha Moon

1969 (Blood Aubade)

for Fred Hampton & Mark Clark

Chairman's head
swims a dream, lover
& unborn son: his crown, wing.
                            How heavy the body
in sleep/death, drag
to vacant doorway, head
a woolen quill, scrawls black
blood @ the hooves of "men."

                            Was it by arm, a fist-
full of hair, yank from the rouge
of the pierced bedroom?
If you know a bullet's wrath—wood splinter,

plaster   )blast(steel drum tap
dance, box spring (catch all) humming
like a hive of bees—you know
the gauge.

                    In the fury—shots
first, no questions, pigs
(black & white) squeal
@ 4:30 a.m.   false aubade.

The bed:
soft alter,
no offer
to our gods.

— Mitchell L.H. Douglas

| 111

kill box

after jon burge

at 91ˢᵗ & cottage grove or viet nam
sixty square mile industrial complex

high yield niggas ravenous concrete
fed dark blood andrew darrell

roy melvin george donald
gerald david darryl one

hundred ninety five black men
and fred mark mumia our sons

the unborn electric shock when
they don't mind screams leave

few clues *it's fun time* kill box
of taxpayers juice another square

blackblack charged crime charred
unforgiving cranked merciless hate

chicago considers all threats
just don't leave any marks

— Quraysh Ali Lansana

In memory of Fong Lee; and for the Lee family, and the Justice for Fong Lee committee

In 2006, Minneapolis Police Officer Jason Andersen shot and killed Fong Lee, a nineteen year old Hmong American. Andersen was awarded a Medal of Valor, though the Lee family and community members allege that Fong Lee was unarmed and the gun found on the scene was planted by police. During a foot chase in North Minneapolis, Andersen shot at Lee nine times, 1 bullet missing, the other 8 hitting Fong Lee as he ran and as he lay dying on the ground.

1.

Community members point out that accusations about Fong Lee's history and character, specifically allegations that he was in a gang, were allowed in court and written about in the press though there was no proof that Lee was ever involved in a gang. However, none of Officer Andersen's history of abuse or judgments of his character was allowed in court.

One of the devil's greatest powers
is to force you to take a deal
that he himself would never take.

2.

Fong Lee was nineteen (*gang member*). I can imagine him (*gang member*) and his (*gang member*) family. They are eating (*gang member*) something that steams and it does not steam like food from this (*gang member*) country, the smell lingers (*gang member*) like home. It is Minnesota so (*gang member*) the lights inside no matter how dim somehow makes (*gang member*) all indoor rooms feel warm. Now its summer and he's fishing with his (*gang member*) friends. They (*gang member*) get on bikes and their (*gang member*) legs drape low, (*gang member*), arms lazy crosses on the handlebars. Their heads lean as they debate the Vikings (*gang member*) and the Twins, slapping absently at the logos (*gang member*) on their caps and (*gang member*) shirts.

Resisting Arrest

3.

Officer Jason Andersen (*hero*) shot Hmong American teenager Fong Lee eight times (*to serve and protect*). A bullet wound in Fong Lee's hand suggests the teenager may have held his hands up in surrender (*decorated officer*) as Officer Andersen (*white*) shot (*Medal of Valor*) him. Andersen was also charged with domestic assault (*peace officer*) by his girlfriend though charges were later dropped (*officer of the law*). Officer Andersen (*police officer*) was also accused of kicking (*hero*) an African American teenager who was on the ground in handcuffs in 2008.

4.

An all-white jury found Officer Anderson not guilty of using excessive force.

Put a blindfold on me
tell me who you fear
and I will tell you
your skin.

5.

I'm wondering when people will care.
If we made your story into a movie about killing dolphins,
perhaps.

6.

I'm eighteen and the brutal cold holsters my hands into the warm solace of my jacket pockets. The police officer snaps his hand to his gun. My pockets are empty. My hands open. Still. My story would have ended in smoke and red snow. If my body lay there, perforated, would I bleed through the holes in his story?

7.

Lost, you turn the car around and see trees stretching up like green-brown fencing up to the blue skies. For a moment you think the woods stretch forever, somewhere close a bubbling stream whispers white kisses across worn rocks, a deer leans its neck down to drink, the velvet moss of a hushed secret world here in your city. But just beyond the neck of scrub trees is the hint of chain-link, the distant ghost silhouette of strip mall, just one step past the shadows of those leaves are railroad tracks running like stitches over broken glass and gravel.

Minnesota Nice: this city hides its scars so well.

8.
All our lives, men with guns.
Chased, in the womb, in the arms
Of our parents.

Our parents
Chased, all our lives,
By men with guns.

In the womb, in our parent's arms
We've run
Chased by men with guns.

(9).
Michael Cho. Cau Thi Bich Tran. John T. Williams.
Tycel Nelson. Oscar Grant. Michael Brown. Chonburi Xiong.
Fong Lee.
May your names be the hymn
wind that sways
police bullets to miss.

— Bao Phi

resisting genocide

everyone is writing poems
about Emmit Till or Amado Diallo
Trayvon Martin or Oscar Grant
Ramarley Graham or so many others

but i
have been writing poems
about young black men
murdered
in the endlessly declared and
undeclared wars of our times

dying while loved
dying while alone
dying while afraid
dying while besieged by enemy
dying while besieged by kin

i have been writing poems

about young black men dying
for about as long as
i have been writing poems

and as i sit here searching
for the right words to pen
in the best places
my mouth is slack
tears held back
as the litany of words
i have already scribed
rolls out beneath me

and the only things
that seem to have changed

are that more of you are dying,
ever younger and more innocent
full of possibilities
that too few seem able to see

and more of you are killing each other
for reasons even you cannot fully explain
unreasoned rage, confusion,
frustration and desire

but the center
of each of my poems
is the same
the killing of
and death of
young black men

i already have stacks of poems
with sharp tipped
blades cutting my heart

black children are killed
without mercy or remorse
without fear of penalty

one black person every
twenty-eight hours
falls from a police officer
security officer, vigilante

while another 8000
die each year
from killing each other

each of these murders
killing our line
ending our future

so i write this poem
for you, the living
you, who we need to offer
more than cautionary advice
telling you to say, "*yes sir*" on demand
keep your hands up and open
stay aware and remember
you *are* a hunted target
always under siege
prejudged as criminal
wrong on account of color
wrong on account of neighborhood
wrong on account of clothes
wrong on account of music
wrong on account of birth

we need to make a way
for all of you
to stride with your smiles
lighting up dark corners
as your neighbors watch out for
the treasure of your inner beauty
and the caprice of your outer style
and the endless potential
of your precious lives

— devorah major

Theory: Evidence of uncertain shifts

Dreams for three nights: I sang *hush* to a wounded man

a cop's gunshots, my brother and he lived. I said a prayer and
a ghost running crowded   woke up calm.
streets and shady hallways.   I severed the angriest part of me
                                   only to have double the raging
                                   weapons grow in its place

— Khadijah Queen

Sonnet Consisting of One Law

You remain free to kill black boys.
You remain free to kill black boys.
You remain free to kill black boys.
You remain free to kill black boys.
You remain free to kill black boys.
You remain free to kill black boys.
You remain free to kill black boys.
You remain free to kill black boys.
You remain free to kill black boys.
You remain free to kill black boys.
You remain free to kill black boys.
You remain free to kill black boys.
You remain free to kill black boys.
You remain free to kill black boys.

— Lynne Thompson

illustrated equation no. 2

something about a look... the shape of things...

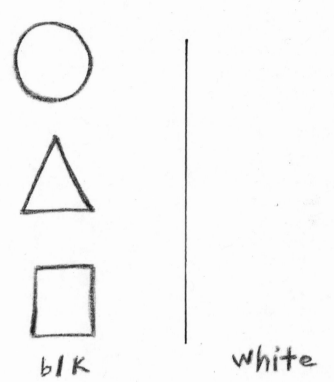

blK   white

there a boat. there a pair
of oars for moving to and
from shore.

blue breaks down. ghosts
emerge from the river,
manifest as fever and fear.

— giovanni singleton

From the Crushed Voice Box of Freddie Gray

I am the Magic Negro
The Black Houdini
Who done it
Done it to him self

I handcuffed my own
Damn self
I threw myself
In the back of the patrol car

My hands shackled
Behind my back
Slaveship cargo
Ago

I am the Magic Negro
The Black Houdini
Who done it
Dooze it to him
Self him black self

See, Ma? No hands!

I snatched the pistol
From the white man's
Mind
From the back of the
Patrol car—

Suck on dis, Houdini!
I grabs the gun
And shoot my
Self in the chest
Neo-colonial style

The autopsy report says
Damn—
Would've been easier

To walk on water
I bet you a quarter
He done shot himself

I am the Magic Negro—
Spineless—

I brokes my own spine
After hogtying myself
Into a pretzel even
Houdini who done it
Would envy

Only to turn myself
Into a human pinball
Rattling around
The steel gullet
Of a Negro pickup truck

Once reserved for newly-
Arrived Potato Famine
New York Irish drunks
Down on their luck—

Me—*moi*—
It is I who was
Othello—
Oh hell no—

Yes—me
The Magic Negro
The Black Houdini
Who done it—
Dooze it all the time

To him self
His own
Damned self

— Tony Medina

Ghazal, After Ferguson

Somebody go & ask Biggie to orate
what's going down in the streets.

No, an attitude is not a suicide note
written on walls around the streets.

Twitter stays lockstep in the frontal lobe
as we hope for a bypass beyond the streets,

but only each day bears witness
in the echo chamber of the streets.

Grandmaster Flash's thunderclap says
he's not the grand jury in the streets,

says he doesn't care if you're big or small
fear can kill a man on the streets.

Take back the night. Take killjoy's
cameras & microphones to the streets.

If you're holding the hand lightning strikes
juice will light you up miles from the streets

where an electric chair surge dims
all the county lights beyond the streets.

Who will go out there & speak laws
of motion & relativity in the streets?

This morning proves a crow
the only truth serum in the street.

— Yusef Komunyakaa

Elegy

for Troy Davis

1.

There was a light rain on the night
of your execution. Wet little pricks
exploding on the skin.
The gears on my bike jammed
so I pedaled crazy-legged, pumping
three times harder, making time.
I glide past a charter bus emptying
in front of the Supreme Court, I double
over at the mostly white choir:
I am Troy Davis / We are Troy Davis.

2.

I am Troy Davis / We Are Troy Davis.
My mother calls hours later,
crying until her eyes swell into beets.
Why are our mothers always crying?
Why am I not crying?
It's become so familiar.
In my boyhood . . .
Rodney King; Billy Clubs;
Loose Nooses; L.A. Riots;
Abner Louima and his attackers:
the police officers shoving a plunger up his rectum;
Amadou Diallo: 41 gun shot wounds;
Echoes of Emmitt Till: Black mothers
unable to recognize their creations.
Men strung on trees left for the crows to suck.
The way Billie Holiday's voice wrinkles
from horror. The gallant South,
the snickering wind.

3.

The gallant South, the snickering wind.
You were lethally injected:
poison entered your veins, stopped your heart,
then your breathing.
I wake up in a cold sweat
hearing you tell the family it wasn't you.
You, Black Socrates. Galileo,
Prisoner to this skin.
I imagine your transition
to the other side with the ancestors.
Afro Blue. I imagine this life different—
not opposed to life, black life.
Not hateful. I imagine
this poem—a proper elegy.
Can you hear that? America singing.
Its trees mock us.
Its wind curses us.
No praying.
God's ears are filled
with cotton.

4.

God's ears are filled with cotton.
Death is my pulse.
I pray daily that I will live to be old,
healthy, but sometimes
I despair. I think
about my mother almost
being thrown on a subway track
carrying me in her belly.
Hearing the metal train car
moving in. Feeling my heart beat.

Wanting to save this black boy
from an early death.
Just one, Lord, spare me one.
I want to teach my daughter
that black doesn't equal death;
and to love her people, all of them,
even the white great-grandmother
who got sick from giving birth
to half-white, all black babies.
And yet, I get quiet each time
we walk by Union Station
that increasingly resembles Monticello.
The homeless: who missed Emancipation
those Negro hymns no longer move me.
Everything is a countdown to
Swing low sweet chariot coming for to carry me home
to be a black mass, riding this skin,
a bomb ticking, soon to expire.

5.

A bomb ticking, soon to expire.
What if we didn't have to die?
What would it mean to live?
What would it mean to give milk
to our own babies?
What would it mean to swim
to the bottom of the ocean,
recovering our bones?
What would it mean to visit
the African burial that is Wall Street?
What does it mean to tell your daughter
We were the first blue chip stock?
That we do not own our children, their lives.
That any motherfucker can point and say

kill that nigger. And it happens. Like that.
Like that. What does it mean to be free
when we've been property longer
than we've been free in this great nation?
What does it mean to say Troy Davis,
my dear brother, I'm Sorry.
A part of me died tonight.
I prayed for the mother ship to come
take me somewhere else.
Do aliens kill each other?
Dear black Socrates,
Galileo:
the planets are spinning.

— Abdul Ali

What They Should Have Done

for Freddie Gray

*When an injury occurs in the back section of the spinal column,
and the individual vertebrae become fractured or dislocated, the
back can be described as broken or fractured... If you are in doubt
about whether a person has a spinal injury, assume that he or she
DOES have one.*
　　　　　　　　　　from http://apparelyzed.com/broken-back.html

No matter what he did or did not do,
they should have kept him safe.
Do not attempt to reposition the neck.

A broken spine is the mass of a broken nation.
Obits in pixels. Slaughter in digital display.
Do not allow the neck to bend or twist.

The force of policing is no match
for any small knife, any reasonable blade.
Check the person's breathing and circulation.

Sidewalks are weapons. Hydrants, too.
Bodies crushed by asphalt, dulled limbs.
DO NOT bend, twist, or lift the person's head or body.

What's the name of the next murdered man?
Next bruised city, town, suburb, alley, store?
You need to check for breathing

but are there breaths left in
bodies that somehow murder themselves?
No matter what he did, said, shed,

no matter what you did or did not do,
they should have kept him safe.
Do not attempt to reposition the neck.

— Allison Joseph

Dear Sandra Bland—

You kept me up last night.
Not in some talk—laugh and/or cry
with a friend until the sun punches the time clock
for another shift kind of way
Not in a ghost hovering above the futon
manner
But as quiet confirmation
The truth, my father once told me—
is simple.
Your wrenching absence—
Sits beside me
Makes me face what I have known
for decades—
(and carried besides joyous,
sometimes goofy things)
That this hate for us
is chronic
the real chronic
And will not willingly surrender
Just as you did not

— Reuben Jackson

"I am broken by the revolt exploding inside me"

Your rage is pomegranates spilling open on ice, is the flute's thin silver seam, is a volcano spitting rivulets of fire to wash clean these corrupt lands. Your rage is solidarity before after & during the hashtag. Your rage is the angel of karma before after & during the video. Your rage throbs tight in your chest against symbologies of sticks & stones & chokes that break ligament & bone. Your rage is the fulcrum of your desire, chimaerae busting out of cages, heart-sparks flying. Your rage gets shit done & it is no joke. Your rage is the luminous gold truth of sunrise, what you sit with long enough to dissolve your fear. Your rage is a checkmate to your compromise. Your rage is heat from a magnifying glass, focused, bursting into flame. Your rage is a cool blue spotlight circling the empty stage. Your rage is the dog who won't lie down for the wrong master, fierce hen who won't be moved till her brood is hatched, moth who unbinds her cocoon & lifts her body toward light. Your rage is a lesson & you learn it as you breathe. Your rage is this holy sword slicing through stone walls. Your rage is a sentence that says what it must, full-stop. Your rage is our dream of a sweeter brighter world. Your rage is this oar treading the sea to steer this ship this gorgeous fucking hot mess goddamn revolution.

Note: The title is a line from "Cruelty" by Namdeo Dhasal, poet and founder of the Dalit Panther movement.

— Minal Hajratwala

The Cascading Body Is Not A Night Sky

In One Form Or Another: Erasure

You cannot riddle a body into night,	You can riddle night
with fireworks, with bullet holes,	with fireworks bullet holes:
with stars wired-up and sparking.	stars red and sparking.
Because the body doesn't bow over	'cause he doesn't bow
the sky as rib cage the heart.	(the sky as rib, cage the heart)
You cannot riddle a body into night.	body into night.
Because the body doesn't bow over	Because he doesn't.
as a hood, as a portaged canoe	a hood, a portaged canoe
with fireworks, with bullet holes	with fire with bull.
rippling through the wood's spine.	rippling rough wood pine
The scars are entry wounds:	The scars are entry wounds:
Stars wired-up and sparking.	Stars red sparking.

— b: william bearhart

We Can't Have Nothing

We can't have nothing. Not our skin. Not our peace. Not our
sanctuary. Can't have nothing. Can't shop, can't swim, can't walk
home. Can't pray. Can't worship. Can't have candy. Can't sit in a
car with friends with the windows down, bathed in bass. Can't
be a free black girl, free black child, free black boy. Can't have
courtesy. Can't ask for help. Can't have nothing. Can't get the
benefit of the doubt. Can't get called by the names we want to be
called. Can't sit in church, pray in church, have a church, mosque,
temple. Can't have nothing. Can't have a nice day, Can't have an
uninterrupted ride home. Can't have a day when you don't have
to look over your shoulder. Can't have nothing. Can't have a day
where you KNOW without a shadow of a doubt the people you
love will come home alive. Can't. Have. Nothing. Can't have a day
when our everything isn't in question. Can't even die without an
"assist". Can't even have a proper burial. Can't even have a memo-
rial that goes untouched. Can't not be followed. In a store. For a
block. For a mile. For a day. For days. For years. For life.
Can't even get an isolated incident.
Can't get an acknowledgement that the race card is manufactured,
         store bought,
and made from our skin.
Can't have nothing.
Can't be a disappeared black girl found safe and in time.
Can't get a disappeared black girl's name read on air.
Can't have an indictment, conviction, blah, blah, blah.
Can't have paid leave, unpaid leave,
break
stop.
Can't have nothing.

— Derrick Weston Brown

Resisting Arrest

| 133

Statement on the Killing of Patrick Dorismond

a petty hoodlum (cop) shot/killed suspect (blackman) after hoodlum (pig) was told by suspect (haitian) that he (junglebunny) was not a drug dealer (nigga). the police commissioner (bounty hunter) referred to suspect (coon) as a "lowlife" (african) though his (aryan) comments were later proven false (white lies). the shooting (genocide) is the third (pattern) in thirteen months (institution) in which plain-clothes officers (gestapo) shot/killed an unarmed man (cheap blood). "I would urge (doubletalk) everyone (oprah) not to jump (dead nigga) to conclusions (acquittals)," mayor guiliani (watchdog) said, "and allow (blind faith) the facts (ethnic cleansing) to be analyzed (spin) and investigated (puppets) without people (darkies) trying to let their biases (racial profiling), their prejudices (welfare queen), their emotions(fuck tha police), their stereotypes (o.j.) dictate the results (status quo)."

— Quraysh Ali Lansana

Yesterday, in the Arms of Unrest

The heart is the stride
of a 1000, marching
a city constructed
of spines.

> (what of a brother, little man
>   watching the night
>   from its edges
>   riddled with rant?)

A curfew
inspires exodus
in real-time; pubescence
occupies every mouth,
furling and unfurling, brick
and mortar, incendiary,
apprehended but not yet broken
fists over verb,
tongues borrowing from
the wind, defiance
in a hoodie's cotton
bloodstream.

A city asks
> (what is a mother's scrape and scratch, the shape
>   of her quail and blues?
>   it is the bolt of skin along her son's scalp,
>   a cervical wound and its peculiar way to talk)

What mechanism turns
flight to blood? seeds
from the hull, shaken
from the gesture, of love
gathered, like a chest, like legs

like breath
held
down

against all doubt,
against the ligature
of a boy's speech, all the air

it takes to plead, beseech, speak
the cacophony we make when we breathe
in the frequencies of rust

The heart is a gymnast
of another's hysteria,
fear another country
lodged between teeth,
while children are schooled
in the passion
of frisk, malice taken
wing in the lunacy
within a uniform's glare

    (bondsman, council and register clerk: recant
        however brief your lament as long as loam.
        Remember instead the way your skin redacts
        its accidents of solitude because

The heart is a bellyache
refuged inside all the verdicts of loss.)

A city negotiates.
But there are no more
first-borns to take the brunt.
Epithets are slung,
soaring Molotovs.

And. The heart becomes a thug
a constituent
for dissidence,
between all streets and their diamond cyclone fence.

The heart is told
to go
to the backrooms
of courage, to find
love (or what comes closest)
entrenched
protesting
in 4/4
time.

Bloodhounds, what hue is the heart?
But the odd pigment of news, the tint of pitch
and discontent, the tarry lining of your father's misery
and all the poison one can spit at love

— Jane Alberdeston Coralin

No Blood On Our Hands or Heart

My heart is not for sale.
Even here in American twilight, even in the crosshairs
Of drones, mercenaries, soldiers or cops.
Asked to choose between a home and health,
Where gray jackals are bold, with no stealth,
Ripping through my scraps of light.

But we intend to stand and fight.
Because we know our hearts are not for sale.
Capitol Hill is for sale; The White House
Is for sale; The NRC, the SEC,
The Pentagon, CIA, FBI, NYPD, PPD, BPD, LAPD,
Military mercenaries and contractors,
Blood-splattered benefactors
Of insane war-on-the-people-without-end,
While character actors

On Capitol Hill are for sale;
The White House is for sale,
The BP watchers and buyers,
The Triple-A credit score liars.
The K Street lawyers and lobbyists
And all those Fox News hires.
Not to mention police who fire on Tahrir Square,
On Walter Scott, and on Wall Street Occupiers

We can't live without water,
Yet, they have sold what we drink to oil drillers,
Gas drillers and frackers.
Who are killing us more than terrorist attackers.

Given our taxes for bankers and bombers,
Missiles and tanks, to kill a child, husband or wife,
For two million Iraqis
Dispatched to the next life.

We want to export something other than war.
We want to build something that does not kill.
In our new world, Peace Be Still.
No more dollars to kill a child, husband or wife.
Bread and roses for Tamir Rice's life, for Rekia Boyd's life.
No blood on my hands or heart.
We won't be quiet.
Let's start.

Who is the terrorist?
Who is the torturer?
Who is the rapist?
Who is the criminal?
Who is the thug?
What police kill the child?
What drones kill with stealth?
What bankster steals the wealth?
And our health? While we obsess over self.

How many wars of roaring beasts over land and oil?
How many Congo hands cut off for rubber
How many Congo women split in two for Coltan.
How many wars for slaves and dollars and gold and diamonds
Now and forever, my heart is not for sale.

I want a no-fly zone over air and water
A no-fly zone over me—no slaughter
A no-fly zone over my womb and vagina.

A no-fly zone over homes, schools and health
Not all for just the one percent, redistribute the wealth!

Listen, you planet vampires,
You fake masters of the universe,
Nobody's walking into your Fourth Reich.

And our hearts are not for sale.
We will export something other than war.
We will build something here that does not kill.
In our new world, Peace Be Still.
No more dollars to kill a child, husband or wife.
Bread and roses for Freddie Gray's snuffed out life.
No blood on our hands or heart.
WE WON'T BE QUIET!
Let's start.

— Esther Iverem

Footnote 666

Law-ordained, ordered arrogance forms
The halos around uniforms, batons, guns,
 Badges, handcuffs, and stuff inform
Novenas for freshly minted killers.
Injustice is all.
This is the way the resolute signs morph
Into rabid symbols after the oaths in blue
Confirm this fraternity shall ruthlessly signify
Innocents are predestined to die.
Injustice is all.
Feral blue uniforms furiously pray
Their prey shall be young, female/male, and black,
Head bowed, silent, hands empty, arms outstretched—
In truth, a crucifix without a cross.
Injustice is all.
This is America, after all, and air is a snarky, bleached privilege.
 Breath of color whose crime is breathing warrants social death.
This is America, the new post-Eden, and all bluebloody uniforms know
Justice is a brazen nuisance, a dangerous God-fearing whore.

— Jerry W. Ward, Jr.

Red Summer, 2015

1
The year
is 2015
Nine holy martyrs are shot
by a man with a scheme
He was nurtured and
weaned on
a textbook of lies
in which slavers and
killers reigned
supreme
Jefferson Davis
Nathan Bedford Forrest
and Robert E. Lee.

2
The devil entered
Vesey's church
disguised as a youth
But the children of god
recognized a hoof
instead of a foot
could smell his soot
but clung to their vow
not to give strangers
the sinner's boot

3
They invited him in
to join them in prayer
and so powerful was their
prayer with its African roots
after Daniel Roof completed
his assignment from hell
He said their prayer
almost got to me
almost turned me
said he

poems to stretch the sky

Almost bought the
the devil to the mourner's
bench
His mind full of bile
he came to defile
A mother played dead
in the blood of her child.

4
A child was shot down
while holding a toy
The police asked questions
but nobody was blamed
The stars in his eyes went
dim in the day
he lay on the pavement
where children played games

5
A man was shot in the
back
while running away
The shooter took aim
as though he were game
the demons are partying
with their buddies, the
fiends, and having a good
time
drinking bad whiskey
and drinking bad wine

6
Red Summer
the year is
2015
For making ends meet
by selling cigs loose
or making a lane change
they will give you the noose
His neck was crushed

in the back of a van
he got "the wild ride"
he could breathe no more
They found her dead on
the jailhouse floor
A grand jury looked
and issued a tome
They blessed the killers
and allowed them to roam.
Go and kill again the
suburbs said,
we got
your back when you shoot
a black in the back

7
When Dorsey got news
that both wife and child were
dead
that's our mood
in this summer of dread
The spirit was his guide
when he wrote that great song
but who is the god
who will take our hand
and who is the god
who will lead us on?

8
"Don't you get weary"
Martin said when he
spoke of his dream
His words have kept us
from drowning in screams
in this bloody summer
of 2015
Where killers and murderers
reign supreme and
demons are partying with their
buddies the fiends, and having
a good time
drinking cheap whiskey
and drinking Ripple

9
You brought down the flag
you all joined hands and
cried
but you still have
highways and buildings
honoring those who
committed high crimes
Who didn't want people to
be free
Jefferson Davis
Nathan Bedford Forrest
and
Robert E. Lee.

— Ishmael Reed

After the Fact

R.I.P. Tyisha Miller 3/3/79-12/28/98

Tyisha,
It was your name
Should have been Katie Lynn
Something Anglo-Protestant,
Not Black,
Someone should have told you that.
Had you been something other than what you were
Maybe Ms. Vermont, Ms. Maine, Ms. Montana
You would have lived.

Should have been blonde
Or brunette
Or Redheaded
Your eyes green
Or blue like siren lights
Then they would have woke you
Never smashed your window
Shot you.
Four policemen, twelve shots in you.

Should not have left your mother's womb
Til she promised you'd be born white.
Should have carried white face paint and
A blond wig in your glove compartment
Would have made you "isolated Incident" proof
Or been born white
Anglo-Protestant, blond, blue-eyed white.
Peggy Sue never got shot by cops
While taking a nap in her car.

— Howard L. Craft

poems to stretch the sky

Changes

woke up again this morning (wonderful surprise gift
at my age), listen to fluttering voices rising up
from the streets below, rhythms of wolof, black harlem
dialects drift inside jangling, enter my ears chattering,
remind of birds outside in the countryside
as they dip, dive, soar, then pause through a sentence of a blue sky
in the shape of commas,

                                    now my telephone rings in
bad news from a weeping relative dropping sadness,
another relative gone down to the bone yard
("people dying today who never died before, verta mae grosvenor
once said), they just gave up the ghost, weary behind all this
stupid shit we got going on here stinking things up
on this out of control planet, people with boatloads of money,
little wisdom, bridges collapsing into dust, amtrak trains wobbling
shooky-shooky before crashing off the rails full of screaming riders,

so my cousin just sent his spirit searching for another light
at the end of a dark tunnel – here in the big apple's subway tunnels
the bright beacon spotlight fixated there in darkness is a train
roaring closer & closer, speeding right into the station
where me & hundreds of other cynical people are waiting –
maybe my cousin was looking for a better space to vibe in, who knows
he ain't here no more to tell us what was depressing his mind,
though it isn't certain he'ill find it where he's going in all that darkness,
but it's definite cuz gonna find maggots & worms down there,
feasting on his flesh & slick suit),

so eye sit here now alone in my airy apartment in harlem,
climb inside my head to escape all this rigmarole,
surrounded by art & light eye filter through my spirit
while my brain dives deep into music through my cocked ears,

paintings on my walls splash colors into my eyeballs,
my heart skips a beat as musical lines open up my imagination
like a can opener & eye feast all kinds of possibilities echoing in there,

leaping into the air full of wondrous musical changes eye walk through,
embrace, amend images, like one that one time in guadeloupe,
eye witnessed rain falling thin as violin strings, heard fingers of wind
creating music from them as if strumming a guitar, heard voices
       born there
reminding me of griots in mali, echoing struggle from the mississippi
       delta,
deeply rooted, moaning the blues, soaked to the bone songs birthed
from wind fingers strumming rain, brought forth saeta, grief,
shooting sorrow music straight as arrows, entered my heart,
like when lament rose from blood soaked soil of andalusia, moors,
where duende pulled manna from deep inside african spritual sadness,

what is it some don't understand hearing grief, sorrow in the blues
(along with happiness, joy there, too), heard in the very marrow
when, flamenco dancers, singers, blues guitarists play,
why is it some cannot comprehend the lost heard there, bone deep,
sadness in the empty, vacant eyes of a once beautiful woman
sprawled naked now, her throat slashed, a scarlet ribbon of blood
angular as a glinting machete blade, dangling from her neck
down to her belly-button – like a rope hanging a female teenager
in india from a remorseless tree – her beauty lying there
in a bed of lime green grass full of sun-flowers nodding
their affirmation of mourning at witnessing her death,
is it the bright sun smiling down that masks horror of this day,
so warm with springtime it makes the heart happy as a child
playing jump-rope, hopping skip to my loo through a field of roses,

what is it about laughter leaping from a child's lips,
wearing the face of a clown, who just shot his mother 10 times
in a fit of rage, makes some think he is a weird comedian,

is it because he appears to be grinning in a photo
 (when perhaps he is garishly leering) & we have no words
to describe, or articulate the mad facial expression of someone
looking like batman's joker after slaughtering 20 children
in their school rooms in connecticut, like those 90 people
machined-gun down in Iceland, while others are seen laughing,
denying the earth is suffering from severe climate change,
did they watch films of mountains of ice fields calving,
collapsing into angry sea water in greenland,

while others refuse to believe blowback is a man dressed all in black,
head to toe, holding up a sharp knife before beheading a man
forced to his knees in the desert dressed in orange, in syria,
then burning another screaming man to death locked in a cage
as the executioner recites scripture from the koran,

why is it some refuse to believe treyvon martin, michael brown,
tamir rice, eric garner, were murdered by white policemen,
while another icy-eyed university cop blew the brains
out of samuel dubose's head in cincinnati, while a white dentist
killed the legendary black mane lion cecil in zimbabwe
just so he could put his massive head up on the wall of his home
in minnesota, while others have come to believe their own
isolating fame, privilege will be shielded by faith,
                              the elixir of boatloads of money,
will deliver them time, space to transform themselves into birds
looking like commas - pauses - high in blue skies & be able
too soar wherever their bank accounts will take them,

in the end it will be imagination in music, language firing poetry,
brushstrokes of painters, creativity in the mind, these things
will free us, serve as launching pads to flight, not the elixir of acquisition,
hoarding trinkets, paper money, countless huge mansions, run-away-egos,
it will be beauty in changes on *kind of blue* we will remember forever,
the tincture of painters, poets, dancers, music, the delta blues, spirituality,

these things will haunt us when we hear voices tonguing through leaves
like kisses bearing sweetness when lips open, tongues meet,
                                        entwine with honey saliva,

love is the fuel after-all to firing imaginations to soar as birds,
become commas pausing sentences,
transforming rhythm in a line of poetry to elegance, heat
through musical alchemy, cadence, grace, beauty,
the power of garcia marquez's sentences, stanzas of neruda, walcott,
wanda coleman, baraka, komunyakaa, then we hear the voice
singing through the poem, inside texts of toni morrison's voice,
haunting, without rigmarole, rancor, pure as the fervor
in leontyne price's voice when she opened her heart, released pure
        beauty,
clear as mile davis' solos haunting "all blues, "blue in green,"
kind of blue, "saeta," "solea" on *sketches of spain*,

when we hear, absorb, understand all this, we will might know
the sweet, powerful elixir of creative, human endeavor, miracles,
the connections we all share here when we understand
changes are rooted in surprise, in a sudden gift of wonder

— Quincy Troupe

the great mystery story is still unsolved.
we cannot even be sure that it has a final solution.

(the) afterlife of corpses in
[A Einstein & Leopold Infeld:
The Evolution of Physics]
a Morse code update primer

+   Forgive me, I had no choice, I begged him, Ladies, I even promised to guide the knife, his first time, professional initiation, never a question of manhood, just some real good stimulation, a little help with ignition, I didn't take it for granted just because I was at Ludlow's Smoker's Palace after hours, an obvious invitation, the way I traipse, I'm rightfully accused of asking for it, how else to make sure I get it, noisy wheel syndrome, but my *it* is a killing, martyr-dumb thing or not, if he's killing me, he's not killing you, so my being on corners is a protection service, and as soon as I'm dead, I won't be there anymore to deflect violations and assassinations onto myself, enjoy it now, pay later, me and my beefed up preference, beefed up refusal to let go of Aileen Wuornos, flip side, inside out side, of one of many kinds of prostitution, rhymes with constitution for a reason, some necessity, some choice, power of, power over a consenting body, power of, power over an antibody, some daring workers work out in advance what the signal will be for arrival at an unspeakable limit, nonverbal signs for *no* and *stop*, hard to misread universals, in addition to face turning blue, eyes rolling, heart stopping, nose bleeding, the most obvious can't-be-mistaken patriotism near death, frequently near death, a fight for freedom, best location in the nation, Ferguson, Baltimore, New York, Cleveland, just getting started, coming to a location near you, where it all converges, denouement, I can't really understand anymore the cowardly aspect of anyone going close to death and hesitating, coming back to where you were, as if you never left, coward, just the feet wet, there are these bruises, maybe these suggestions of psychosis, they can emerge when anything anyone can do is extended far enough, there's a path there, but I haven't been able to get close to it yet, guide me, I am not teasing you, Killer, you can take me all the way, till death do we part, hero, otherwise, most of the time the sex is routine, it adds up unremarkable, the mechanics, the remarkable is exception, which could be to feel nothing if nothing is felt only once, I don't know what changes when you're doing it for the money, for a living, even when you're not, you don't always feel the target highest of high feelings, if that's necessarily the point, there's always the exercise benefit, more or less, the risk of disease, risk of abrasion, risk of success, empire of self-made women, maybe the money puts you over the top, one percent of you in penthouses (all the time), the math of emotion, the feelings that accompany accumulation, everybody, my killer included, potentially in the emotionally overtaxed bracket, I won't get any money that I can use for my murder, I'm not exploring the psychology of calling it a trick, a dupe, a pulling of wool, I too plan to sell my body, (*effects of MS, of course—that disease alone can kill you*), but I prefer Hector's intimacy, the touching he'll have to do to kill me well, profits to go to charity just like the benefits of my murder go to the charity of sparing another woman from being on the slab, the life I save, there's not a lot of admitted interest in the afterlife of corpses, most are put in the ground, indirect nutrients, or are burned, smoke and ashes, dispersal in the air, floating, drifting, the superficial Zen at the end of it all, residue, aftermath of the rapture, the loved one off the ground, not the table in a séance, a casket is a derailed subway car, but once the power's back on, once I'm dead, I'll be out of your way, my killer will be off the street, you know to watch me, you know you can catch him, finger him, fulfillment of dream of fingering the fossil flute of spine, *yes, yes,* you tend to be law enforcement's best extended set of eyes, your clientele is so comprehensive, from so many spheres and arenas, trick universe, you don't have to thank me for this service, by extension I'm one of your clients, just short of psychosis, no matter what else I sleep with, I sleep with this knowledge too, once I'm dead, you won't ever have to thank me, and if you don't, so what, sometimes you're paid to beg, one of the easiest dog tricks, the puppy can learn it, the older bitch and dog, almost as old as wolf, the pimp is one evolution of shepherd, my killer is from another line, none of us are daughters of Abel, but I am starting to feel desperate, it should have happened by now, my big break, my cracked skull, broken neck, every day, every hour, every minute or so, every few seconds, a woman is assaulted, what's wrong with the Ludlow environment, secondary nature, how did it get this exemption, here I am, cautious killer, toss the caution, take a swing at me, use the knife tip as stainless tongue proxy, *cock proxy,* come on, come on already, what's the matter big boy, I'm waiting for you, would it help if I called you *daddy,* that would not help me, where's a good old fashioned knife-thrower-without-limits mentality when you need one? –I'm sorry I need it only once, but surely you're a normal champion of one night time standing still, *yes, yes,* a bullet taking forever, my rapid fall slowed down to ballet, swan lake, Siegfried comes of age, hunts birds in the evening, Odette pleads for the swans' survival, a deal in the dark, *yes,* good only in the dark, *yes,* the double dark of Odile, the double dark in which a man and his swan drown, just as scripted, Tchaikovsky knew what he wanted from the music, what's a wingless girl to do to get what she wants from a man who's able to give it and then some, try the buzz-saw slipper on my foot, *yes,* please, put me to sleep with a bear-trap kiss, if you're not up to full-blown iron maiden, how about it, I'll pay you, give you my PIN: 7715 upside down is easily twisted to kill, something less than a man can twist that, ordinary bender of spoons, reach me at 5455437 on the phone: call me every hour on the hour, spell out *kill her* all day long, redial, reload, I spell it out every day with my footsteps, my tap dance, stiletto dictation, highly specialized Morse code update, war hero revival, post traumatic stress syndrome, collateral damage, déjà vu, do what some did at Mai Lai, do what some did at Nanking, Fallujah, Abu Ghraib, do what some did in Birmingham, at Manassas, Ferguson, Baltimore, New York, Cleveland, on campus, I will not press charges, I'll be as quiet as a mouse at your feet, cat drop, as more surfaces, you are inside me, seeking the prehistoric *bling-bling* of my spine, interlocked heavy necklace, the vertebrae like ossified roses, my death glistens, you catch a hard bouquet, open a treasure chest, treasure breasts =

— Thylias Moss

Dying of Ignorant Talk While Taking Bullets

we do not hear the pain of others,
nor listen to the under-doings of
a people, a nation, of empire.
it is not the bullets to the head,
chokeholds on the neck,
or the piercing of the heart of a
twelve-year-old boy in cleveland.
it is not the 110 shot to death in march
by first responders across the nation
    dancing in fear,
    dying of ignorant talk,
    close-eyed to the rape of children
    pimped by prosperity ministers, politicians, bankers and wall
street.

it is not the nightly news with
"if it bleeds it leads" or talk-show hosts
who can't write or speak a coherent paragraph
but can lie, throw hatred, sell sugar, used cars,
enemies list and champion the ideas of the
monied-few running in white fright and flight
miles ahead of the poor, ignorant, unheard & suffering majority.

the monied-few buy
people who vote against themselves,
people who find comfort in whiteness and witless sound blast,
multiple homes & yachts, offshore accounts,
exclusive clubs, negative taxes, private education,
tripled filtered water, beef and yes people ordering
the 47 congressional traitors to sign a letter to the
leadership of Iran against our own president and country.

bullets not only come encased in lead
they arrive as anti-intellectualism disguised as knowledge,
in legislation from ALEC[1] to legally
steal federal land, fix taxes protecting the
richest of the one percent plutocrats and as
anti-national healthcare as long as congress people are covered[2]

 bullets penetrate the ugliest in
children without family, love and security,
and teenagers who only listen to each other, the
hot wind of corporate shoe makers and the
bling, bling of rappers who can't spell responsibility,
recognize the N word for what it actually is, or
acknowledge the game and gangs they've lost to

bullets eliminate the masses with a
bought, sold and compromised corporate media,
test-fixing educators,
ill informed and conflicted politicians,
doctors betraying their "do no harm" oath,
as they and the monied-few sabotage the
good in good, the yes in quality and the
fading smiles of 8-year-olds as
grandfathers and mothers greet the
unsuspected at walmart feeding their
hard worked money to the gigantic suck machine of
goods from china, india and south america as
u.s. factories close by the thousands as the leaders
blame the people for the bankruptcy of states, cities and
washed out ideas of wall street, banks and a government
living on punctured rafts unable to wash itself of
lobbyists, finance, pacs and the soiled
beliefs of whiteness and the work less wealthy all
hiding in private jets, newly acquired islands and
well stocked bomb shelters from the sixties.

---

1 American Legislative Exchange Council
2 Senator Ted Cruz of Texas

there is a giant hole in the u.s. constitution
written three centuries ago for a nation built on and by
enslaved africans, indentured poor whites & three-fifths of a per-
son clauses
benefiting the white-gods of money and property.
there is colossal hypocrisy in the nation's constitution
that protects in principal what governments deny in practice,
whose responses to evil is medieval in empowering a
ruler-ship who could not find justice in a one word dictionary and
marvels daily at their work of cloning a people
who would much rather believe than think.

— Haki R. Madhubuti

Many Thousand-Thousands Gone

They are not just
statistics, not just numbers.
They are our grown kids and grandkids.
They are our heartbeats. Let us say their names:

Morris Pina, Trayvon Martin, Eric Garner,
Michael Brown.
Tamir Rice, Akai Gurley, Rumain Briston,
Ezel Ford,
Timothy Russell, Malissa Williams, Sandra Bland…

BLACK LIVES MATTER!

Hey, they kill unarmed black girls and women, too.
Hell yes, they do!

Though one would have been
too many, how many children cried
and died on the coastward trek in coffles?
How many soon died of diet, shock, or the dark curtain
of depression in the barracoons like Goree? How many died
of "flux" in the suffocating hold of the slave ship *Gracia De Dios*
during the four centuries of the Atlantic slave trade. God, how many?

BLACK LIVES MATTER!!

How many with their last moans
"flew" home to Africa during the first soul-chilling snow
after auction block? How many
galloped away in the night on a white, red-speckled horse
named Consumption? How many
tiny bundled ones froze or burned up with fever in parents' arms
on The Underground Railroad?

BLACK LIVES MATTER!!!

It kills and kills. How many
Emmett Tills have we had?
If it was or is only one child,
one would be too many.

So why are so many of those uniformed in blue hues
forcing so many lethal overdoses of "Service and Protection"
onto those who in any clothes are uniformly blues people?
What is it in some that makes them kill our kids and grandkids
on sight, on site makes them irrationally angry
or full of fright, gives them excuse to abuse
their uncivil civic might?

BLACK LIVES MATTER!!!!

What does it profit them to create this mass
incarceration state at such a rate? Well, hell, what profited
from its holdings in slave ships? What got rich off the quarters
behind Mount Vernon and Monticello and waxed fat from fields
of indigo-dyed cotton blues? And still does by nixing really righteous raps'
raw anger at The State of Things?

The ugly id of Amerika kills and kills unarmed kids
with impunity, as if with some kind of diplomatic immunity. The hate kills,
wrongfully outright murders boys and men of color it cannot incarcerate
in this mass-prisons-for-profits state. We hold *these* truths to be self-evident:

Morris,Trayvon, Eric, Malcolm, Michael, Tamir, Akai, Rumain,
Ezel, Tony, Timothy, Malissa…

BLACK LIVES MATTER!!!!!

Who are the accomplices in all of this? Those of us unwilling to fight
to change a system that profits from crack and heroin addiction,
from under-funded public schools, reversed voting rights,
The State-of-Hate's legislatures that will not enact
laws to prosecute cops for murders of unarmed
citizens, from ghettos, mass joblessness,
from mass jailings' labor camps ...
and so around and around
it goes. And so go we.
See?

BLACK LIVES MATTER!!!!!!

Though one would be too many,
how many unarmed black boys, men, girls, women
of color have been copped, objectified, commodified wrong-
fully outright killed? Many, many

MILLIONS!!!!!!!

Millions by the dozens, millions by the score.
Come on good people, let us make sure there are
no more, no more. Power To The People!!!

BLACK LIVES MATTER!
BLACK LIVES MATTER!!
BLACK LIVES MATTER!!!

— Everett Hoagland

Why No Flowers for Africa?

Parisians, Syrians, the Lebanese, the Kenyans,
the Nigerians, Malians, Indonesians and the Burkinabé
all suffer the consequences of war and fundamentalism
They sit at cafes, go to concerts, attend soccer matches,
go to school, stay in a hotel, trying to escape for a better life
They see family and friends being killed

Parisians and tourists
are told to stay indoors
They can't live their everyday lives
We are asked to sympathize with them
because they can't see the Mona Lisa at the Louvre,
sip espresso at Le Deux Magots,
load up on baguettes on the Champs-Elysees
and see the views from the top of the Eiffel Tower
Their children are caught in the middle of a fight
they did not cause
The sins of colonialism
visited upon its children out to hear music
What are the French doing in independent Africa?
Looting minerals, food and art

The Eiffel Tower may be lit in the colors
of the Malian flag
but the Police Nationale
surround African immigrants
selling tiny knickknacks to tourists
at that same Eiffel Tower
and the national gendarmerie
send them
to Charles de Gaulle Airport
from where they are kicked
out of "the city of lights"

All we hear about on the news are the attacks in Paris
Why don't we hear as much about attacks in Syria, Nigeria,
Kenya, Mali, Lebanon, Indonesia, and Burkina Faso?
Beirut got attacked the day before Paris,
Nairobi seven months before,
and Nigeria, Mabako, Indonesia and Bukina Faso afterwards
What about ISIS raping women and children in their camps
or Boko Haran kidnapping two hundred girls and
killing thirty people in a suicide bombing?

People said, "Je suis Paris"
and "Prayers for Paris"
but no "I am Beirut,"
"I am Mabako,"
"I am Nairobi,"
"I am Jakarta,"
and "I am Burkino Faso"
They made the French flag
their profile picture on Facebook
but where are the sightings
of the Nigerian, Malian, Kenyan,
Syrian, Lebanese, Indonesian
or Burkinabé flags?

On the news we watched
a drowned Syrian child
washed ashore near the Turkish resort of Bodrum
or families walking hundreds of miles to Hungary
to catch a train to Austria or Germany
only to be turned back.
Some states won't allow refugees
for fear of terrorist attacks
or in their words, "The US not wanting Syrian refugees here
is not based not on fear,
it is based on wisdom and knowledge.

We should admit only proven Christians."
How do they prove they are Christian?
Maybe mounting a crucifix at checkpoints
to swear their devotion?

A presidential candidate
wants to I.D. Muslim citizens
and shut down mosques
The black president is called a
"sissy," "wuss" and a "petulant child"
(translation: the updated Jim Crow term for "boy")
He is called the first female
as well as Black president
for urging restraint
even though the terrorism in Europe
was done by home grown terrorists
Someone said to me,
"They don't consider the Syrians people.
They consider them contraband."
Which immigrant families have caused more terror
Syrian families or the Bush family?

When the attacks happened in Beirut,
Nigeria, Kenya, Mali, Indonesia
and Burkino Faso
there were no national anthems sung,
no buildings lit up in the countries' colors,
no comparisons to 9-11,
no moments of silence,
no 24 hour news cycle
on CNN or MSNBC,
just their "experts"
who spend their lives in green rooms
sampling free doughnuts and coffee
instead of interviews with civilians
presidents, prime ministers,
or experts from the countries involved

Why is a life in France
worth more grief and anger
than a life in Nigeria, Mali
Kenya, Lebanon,
Indonesia and Burkino Faso?
Where are the world's candles,
the vigils, the anthem-singing,
the hashtags, the letters,
the flowers for these victims?

— Tennessee Reed

Chicago

An open casket funeral
Till's home
RIP blue caskets
RIP Till
That boy down the street
Sirens an anthem
House music playing over a crying mother
Insert death totals over Negro Spiritual
Insert a funeral so t'd they knocked over Jojo's casket
The floor
Insert Jojo's casket
Insert Jojo
Unkill the boy
Unconsole his mother
Remove the redlining and the train named after it
Desegregate the most segregated city
Didn't see the white people near home
Our block incubated in racism
Fertilized Jon Burge
Mothers who fertilized four fetuses black and boy
Scars and skin
Know the fall from the slide
Know the fall from concrete
Know how to get up
That chicken
That man
Learned Harold's mild sauce
Know separation of chicken
Wings
Brown boys love chicken covered red
Know this
Brown chicken covered in red
This brown covered in red
This brown boy covered in red
Brown boys covered in red

—Onam Lansana

muh-tem-suh-koh-sis or
"When she insists on coming back as a poem"

When black people die
I become a ghostwriter.
I complete their sentences.
I am careful to give them
And not death the credit.
When black people die
I become a preacher.
Allllll black deaths are prophetic.
Allllll black deaths warn.
Allllll black deaths rattle.
Allllll black deaths are vatic utterances.
When black people die
I become a poet.
And because you can not use
Racism, domestic terrorism, or state violence
In a poem when black people die,
I become the sound of a churning truth,
The coming to terms,
The new name to call this lie,
I am the nomenclature,
I am the failure of words,
I am the mouth with the bitter taste,
The cyanide in the cherry pie,
The refusal to swallow death
Despite its insistence,
I am the knowing
That when the sweet has stopped,
The poem's soul is evolving,
And reincarnating in my mouth,
I am the coming back
I am the Lifetime after a lifetime
Of revisions because I refused
To return as hate.

— Marvin K. White

Dismantling Grief

is never a straightforward thing. Start
with a handful of earth, scattered over the wrapped
body lowered into the ground. Move

back to when you were tying your shoe laces
before the phone rang—the *Allo?*, the silence.
"Are we all martyrs?" writes Darwish.

Months after the burial, he will come back
to ask about the bullets, the holes in his chest. Tell him,
"You were eating falafel on the street." Try

to stay still until almost nothing is left
but the sound of water inside the building walls.
The beauty of sunsets will hurt. Fade

the red. Like a matchstick,
you will break, burn. Go back
to that afternoon when you were both ten,

learning how to make a circle. Remember
how he taught you to steady your hand. Go out
on the balcony. Sip your morning coffee in the cold, look—

the paper on the parked car says "For Sale"
and Julia is singing, "I pray for you." This is a good day
to run. Your shoes are in the closet. Get them.

— Zeina Hashem Beck

Poetry Workshop after the Verdict

for Trayvon Martin

Morning lights your four windows,
and you wake. It is, already, another day.
You stumble, befuddled, into the bathroom,
so white it's like you're inside the moon.
You look in the mirror, then turn away;
better to just leave. Get your body out the door
and into the blue day. You follow the brown—
sparrow, maybe?—perched outside on the rail
like a guide. Bring everything already packed
inside your skin—a dead brown boy and his free killer,
his judge and jury of women, the six *not guilty* bells
clanging again and again in your weary ear.
No, that's your alarm; it's time to be a poet.
You bring your pen and notebook, your poet's eye.
You try to follow instructions: *Write what you see.*
It's simple. You walk down the road,
safe in your pack of poets—women, white.
(You do not write this in your notebook.)
Instead, your eyes find and follow the lines
that run everywhere—across the street,
up the railings, across windows and shutters,
siding, shingled rooftops— parsing the landscape
into cells. Your white journal pages, ruled.
You write down all the signs: *Closed;*
Peter's Property Management; Not for public use;
These dunes aren't made for walking; stop.
But you cannot stop. You follow the wind,
ripe with salt and already-sweaty bodies.
You see a pile of beached boats lumped

like bodies in a mass grave; a stone wall drowning
while sleepy dories drift by; sun-bleached
stumps, slowly going to rot; You see
the sun marking time as it slips higher
and higher, the day stretching overhead,
last night's dark already memory. You see
an American flag, and below it, the reddening back
of a white boy lying face down on the sand,
his body the opposite of a chalk outline. You write:
the light skitters brilliantly atop the bay's piercing
blue. You write: *A boy, his light hair lightening to gold,*
his body, so still, still breathing. You write: *Not guilty,*
Not guilty, Not guilty, Not guilty, Not guilty, Not guilty.

— Lauren K. Alleyne

"Teach Us to Number Our Days"

In the old neighborhood, each funeral parlor
is more elaborate than the last.
The alleys smell of cops, pistols bumping their thighs,
each chamber steeled with a slim blue bullet.

Low-rent balconies stacked to the sky.
A boy plays tic-tac-toe on a moon
crossed by TV antennae, dreams

he has swallowed a blue bean.
It takes root in his gut, sprouts
and twines upward, the vines curling
around the sockets and locking them shut.

And this sky, knotting like a dark tie?
The patroller, disinterested, holds all the beans.

August. The mums nod past, each a prickly heart on a sleeve.

— Rita Dove

In Two Seconds

Tamir Rice, 2002 - 2014

the boy's face
climbed back down the twelve-year tunnel

of its becoming, a charcoal sunflower
swallowing itself. Who has eyes to see,

or ears to hear? If you could see
what happens fastest, unmaking

the human irreplaceable, a star
falling into complete gravitational

darkness from all points of itself, all this:

the held loved body into which entered
milk and music, honeying the cells of him:

who sang to him, stroked the nap
of the scalp, kissed the flesh-knot

after the cord completed its work
of fueling into him the long history

of those whose suffering
was made more bearable

by the as-yet-unknown of him,

playing alone in some unthinkable
future city, a Cleveland,

whatever that might be.
Two seconds. To elapse:

the arc of joy in the conception bed,
the labor of hands repeated until

the hands no longer required attention,
so that as the woman folded

her hopes for him sank into the fabric
of his shirts and underpants. Down

they go, swirling down into the maw
of a greater dark. Treasure box,

comic books, pocket knife, bell from a lost cat's collar,
why even begin to enumerate them

when behind every tributary
poured into him comes rushing backward

all he hasn't been yet. Everything
that boy could have thought or made,

sung or theorized, built on the quavering
but continuous structure

that had proceeded him sank into
an absence in the shape of a boy

playing with a plastic gun in a city park
in Ohio, in the middle of the afternoon.

When I say *two seconds,* I don't mean the time
it took him to die. I mean the lapse between

the instant the cruiser braked to a halt
on the grass, between that moment

and the one in which the officer fired his weapon.
The two seconds taken to *assess the situation.*

And though I believe it is the work
of art to try on at least the moment
and skin of another,

for this hour I respectfully decline.

I refuse it. May that officer
be visited every night of his life
by an enormity collapsing in front of him

into an incomprehensible bloom,
and the voice that howls out of it.

If this is no poem then...

But that voice — erased boy,
beloved of time, who did nothing
to no one and became

nothing because of it — I know that voice
is one of the things we call poetry.
It isn't to his killer he's speaking.

— Mark Doty

Skit: Sun Ra Welcomes the Fallen

Jupiter means anger. Sun Ra does not. Sun Ra dances the Cake
Walk on Saturn's pulpy eyes. If you believe that, I'll tell you
another one. The first is 13 and the next is 20. They were not good
boys but they were boys. They were boys who died for this thing
or that. The next was 16 and the last was 18. One had a cell phone.
One had a gun. On earth, a goose opens its chest to a sound. The
goose takes the bullet this way. A sacrifice denied to the wind
since there is no such thing as sacrifice anymore having
succumbed to fever and the millennium. The bullet is all
consequence. Sun Ra refuses red—long and high, low and deep.
His arms are long enough to embrace them.

— Ruth Ellen Kocher

A Small Needful Fact

Is that Eric Garner worked
for some time for the Parks and Rec.
Horticultural Department, which means,
perhaps, that with his very large hands,
perhaps, in all likelihood,
he put gently into the earth
some plants which, most likely,
some of them, in all likelihood,
continue to grow, continue
to do what such plants do, like house
and feed small and necessary creatures,
like being pleasant to touch and smell,
like converting sunlight
into food, like making it easier
for us to breathe.

— Ross Gay

#IfIDieinPoliceCustody

If I die in police custody
Know that I am not Houdini
That hole in my chest
Did not magically appear

Regardless of my hands
Cuffed behind my back
That I preferred my blood
Inside my body instead
Of pouring through

Powder-burned flesh
Pooling at my feet
In the backseat
Of some patrol car

If I die in police custody
Don't let my bone fragments
Puzzle the public
When the police insist
I reached for a gun

That if I had magic powers
I would not use them
To end my little life
But to save it

— Tony Medina

Philadelphia: Spring, 1985

1.

*/a phila. Fireman reflects after
seeing a decapitated body in the MOVE ruins/*

to see those eyes
orange like butterflies
over the walls.

I must move away
from this little-ease
where the pulse
shrinks into itself
and carve myself in white.

O to press the seasons
and taste the quiet juice
of their veins.

2. */memory/*

a.

Thus in a varicose town
where eyes splintered the night with glass
the children touched at random
sat in places where legions rode.

And O we watched the young birds
stretch the sky
until it streamed white ashes
and O we saw mountains lean on seas
to drink the blood of whales
then wanter dumb with their wet bowels.

b.

Everywhere young
faces breathing in crusts.
breakfast of dreams.
The city, lit by a single fire,
followed the air into order.
And the Sabbath stones singed our eyes
with each morning's coin.

c.

Praise of a cureless death they heard
without confessor;
Praise of cathedrals
pressing their genesis from priests;
Praise of wild gulls who came and drank
their summer's milk,
then led them toward the parish snow.

How still the spiderless city
The earth is immemorial in death.

— Sonia Sanchez

A Poem for Freddie Gray, Baltimore

Each heart its own vessel, each wish
a summation of a day not even that heart
can know, and here now, in this moment,
this pulled out flesh of time, undone is
what it comes to be, undone to do again,
somewhere in the rolled back eyes
of repeating what we call history when
history cannot be repeated. We make
new memories each time we breathe,
and breathing fire we remove care
from the core of what we call love because
we have come to believe no one cares,
as the air is filled with meaningless bits
of meaning cut to shreds, walked on,
forgotten. If tomorrow never comes,
it is the fault of some misplaced moon
and not the failure of what we know
is human, what we know has mind and
wish and hope carved out of spaces
where we learned to live despite hatred.

— Afaa Michael Weaver

I Give You Back

I release you, my beautiful and terrible
fear. I release you. You were my beloved
and hated twin, but now, I don't know you
as myself. I release you with all the
pain I would know at the death of
my children.

You are not my blood anymore.

I give you back to the soldiers
who burned down my house, beheaded my children,
raped and sodomized my brothers and sisters.
I give you back to those who stole the
food from our plates when we were starving.

I release you, fear, because you hold
these scenes in front of me and I was born
with eyes that can never close.

I release you
I release you
I release you
I release you

I am not afraid to be angry.
I am not afraid to rejoice.
I am not afraid to be black.
I am not afraid to be white.
I am not afraid to be hungry.
I am not afraid to be full.
I am not afraid to be hated.
I am not afraid to be loved.

to be loved, to be loved, fear.

Oh, you have choked me, but I gave you the leash.
You have gutted me but I gave you the knife.
You have devoured me, but I laid myself across the fire.

I take myself back, fear.
You are not my shadow any longer.
I won't hold you in my hands.
You can't live in my eyes, my ears, my voice
my belly, or in my heart my heart
my heart my heart

But come here, fear
I am alive and you are so afraid
                                        of dying.

— Joy Harjo

The Poets

Jane Alberdeston Coralin, co-author of the novel, *Sister Chicas,* is an English professor at the University of Puerto Rico-Arecibo. Her work has been published in various literary journals and anthologies, including *Sargasso: A Journal of Caribbean Literature, Language and Culture* and *Rattle: Poetry for the 21st Century.*

Abdul Ali is the author of *Trouble Sleeping,* winner of the 2014 New Issues Poetry Prize, selected by Fanny Howe. He's the recipient of numerous fellowships and accolades, including a two-time recipient of a Literature fellowship from the DC Commission on the Arts and Humanities.

Lauren K. Alleyne is the author of *Difficult Fruit.* Her work has earned several honors and awards, most recently the Picador Guest Professorship in Literature at the University of Leipzig, Germany and a 2014 Iowa Arts Council Fellowship. Alleyne is the Poet-in-Residence, and an Assistant Professor of English at the University of Dubuque.

T.J. Anderson III is the author of *Cairo Workbook, River to Cross, Notes to Make the Sound Come Right: Four Innovators of Jazz Poetry,* the spoken-word CD *Blood Octave* and the chapbook *At Last Round Up.* He lives with his family in Roanoke, Virginia, and teaches at Hollins University. tanderson@hollins.edu.

Jabari Asim is acting director of the MFA program in creative writing at Emerson College. His books include *Only The Strong,* a novel, and *A Taste of Honey,* a story collection. He is executive editor of the Crisis magazine, published by the NAACP and was a *Washington Post Book World* editor from 1996 to 2007.

b: william bearhart is a direct descendent of the St Croix Chippewa Indians of Wisconsin, an MFA candidate in the Lo Rez program at the Institute of American Indian Arts, and currently works as a poker dealer in a small Wisconsin casino when not writing or editing. His work can be found or is forthcoming in *Bloom, Cream City Review, North American Review, PANK, Prairie Schooner,* and *Tupelo Quarterly* among others.

Zeina Hashem Beck is a Lebanese poet whose first collection, *To Live in Autumn* (The Backwaters Press, 2014) has won the Backwaters Prize and was a runner up for the Julie Suk Award. Twice Pushcart-prize nominee, her work has appeared in *Ploughshares, Poetry Northwest, 32 Poems, The Common,* and *Magma,* among others.

Tara Betts is the author of *Break the Habit,* and *Arc & Hue,* as well as the chapbooks *7 x 7: kwansabas* and *THE GREATEST!: An Homage to Muhammad Ali.* Her poems appear in numerous journals and anthologies, including *POETRY, Gathering Ground, Bum Rush the Page, Villanelles, The Break Beat Poets, Octavia's Brood: Science Fiction Stories from Social Justice Movements* and *GHOST FISHING: An Eco-Justice Poetry Anthology.*

Roger Bonair-Agard is author of three collections of poems, the most recent of which, *Bury My Clothes,* was long listed for the National Book Award. He teaches Creative Writing with Free Write Jail Arts at the Cook County Juvenile Temporary Detention Center.

Derrick Weston Brown is the author of *Wisdom Teeth.* He holds an MFA in Creative Writing from American University and is a graduate of the Cave Canem and VONA summer workshops. His work appears in numerous journals, including *Warpland, Mythium, JoINT, Tidal Basin Review* and the *Little Patuxent Review.*

Jericho Brown is the author of *Please,* which won the American Book Award, and of *The New Testament,* which won the Anisfield-Wolf Book Award. He is an associate professor in English and creative writing at Emory University in Atlanta.

Mahogany L. Browne is a Cave Canem & Poets House alum, publisher of Penmanship Books & Poetry Program Director of the Nuyorican Poets Café, educator and an activist. She is the author of *Smudge* and *Redbone.*

Ana Castillo is a celebrated and distinguished poet, novelist, short story writer, essayist, editor, playwright, translator and independent scholar. Her bestselling, award-winning books include *Give It to Me, So Far from God, The Guardians, Peel My Love Like an Onion, I Ask the Impossible, The Mixquiahuala Letters, Loverboys* and *Sapogonia,* a *New York Times* Notable Book of the Year.

Ching-In Chen is author of *The Heart's Traffic* and co-editor of *The Revolution Starts at Home: Confronting Intimate Violence Within Activist Communities*. A Kundiman, Lambda and Callaloo Fellow, they are part of the Macondo and Voices of Our Nations Arts Foundation writing communities, and are senior editor of *The Conversant*. www.chinginchen.com

James Cherry is the author of *Loose Change*. He holds an MFA in creative writing from the University of Texas at El Paso and is the author of a novel, a collection of short fiction and three volumes of poetry. Cherry lives in Tennessee where he teaches poetry to At-Risk youth. www.jamesecherry.com

Howard L. Craft is a poet, playwright, and arts educator. He is the author of *Across The Blue Chasm* (Big Drum Press). His plays include *FREIGHT: The Five Incarnations of Abel Green*. He teaches children in public and private schools, and adults through the North Carolina Writers Network, Duke Center for Documentary Studies and other organizations. He has received grants from the NC Arts Council, the Durham Arts Council and is a two-time recipient of the NC Central University New Play Project.

Kwame Dawes, Ghanaian-born Jamaican poet, is the award-winning author of sixteen books of poetry (most recently, *Wheels*, 2011) and numerous books of fiction, non-fiction, criticism and drama. He is the Glenna Luschei Editor of *Prairie Schooner*, and a Chancellor's Professor of English at the University of Nebraska. He also teaches in the Pacific MFA Writing program. His most recent book is *Duppy Conqueror: New and Selected Poems*.

Joel Dias-Porter (aka DJ Renegade) is the largest pigeon to ever sit on a bench on the Atlantic City Boardwalk. He is widely published on the Internet of idiots and the skin of a few dead trees. Also, powdered mini donuts.

LaTasha N. Nevada Diggs, writer, vocalist and curator, is the author of TwERK. A Cave Canem fellow, she has published in *Black Renaissance Noir, Fence, Palabra, Ploughshares, Jubilatand LA Review,* among others. She has received grants and awards from New York Foundation for the Arts, The Jerome Foundation, the National Endowment for the Arts, US Japan Friendship Commission and Creative Capital. She is a native of Harlem.

Mark Doty's nine books of poems include *Fire to Fire: New and Selected Poems*, which won the National Book Award for Poetry in 2008, and *Deep Lane* (Norton, 2016). He teaches at Rutgers University and lives in New York City.

Mitchell L. H. Douglas is the author of *Cooling Board: A Long-Playing Poem*, and *\blak\ \al-fə bet*, which won the Lexi Rudnitsky Editor's Choice Award, leading to its publication by Persea Books in 2013. He is a founding member of the Affrilachian Poets, a Cave Canem graduate, and poetry editor for *Pluck!: The Journal of Affrilachian Arts & Culture*. He teaches at Indiana University-Purdue University Indianapolis where he directs the creative writing program.

Rita Dove is Commonwealth Professor of English at the University of Virginia in Charlottesville. Her many distinctions include a Heinz Award in the Arts and Humanities, a Common Wealth Award, a National Humanities Medal and the Pulitzer Prize for her poetry collection, *Thomas & Beulah*. She is author of *On the Bus with Rosa Parks*, a finalist for the National Book Critics Circle Award and *Sonata Mulattica, winner of a Hurston-Wright Award; Through the Ivory Gate*, a novel; and the play *The Darker Face of the Earth*, which was produced at the Kennedy Center for the Performing Arts in Washington, D.C

Cornelius Eady holds the Miller Chair at the University of Missouri-Columbia. His many books include *Brutal Imagination* and *Hardheaded Weather*. He is a founder of the Cave Canem workshop and sings, plays and records with his band Rough Magic.

Kelly Norman Ellis is a mother, poet and professor. She is chairperson of the English Department at Chicago State University and author of two poetry collections, *Tougaloo Blues* and *Offerings of Desire*.

Thomas Sayers Ellis is a poet and photographer. The author of *The Maverick Room* and *Skin, Inc: Identity Repair Poems* (Graywolf Press). He co-founded The Dark Room Collective and is a co-founding member of Heroes Are Gang Leaders, a literary protest band of musicians and poets. His poems have appeared in *Pluck!, Poetry, The Paris Review, The Nation* and *Best American Poetry* 1997, 2001, 2010 and 2015.

Martín Espada is the author of more than 15 books as a poet, editor, essayist and translator. Professor of English at the University of Massachusetts, Amherst his books include, *A Mayan Astronomer in Hell's Kitchen, Alabanza: New and Selected Poems, 1982–2002* (2003), *The Republic of Poetry* and *The Trouble Ball*. Espada won the Paterson Award for Sustained Literary Achievement with the publication of *Alabanza;* which also named an American Library Association Notable Book of the Year.

Adam Falkner is an instructor of English and Education at Columbia University's Teachers College and Vassar College. Founder and Executive Director of the Dialogue Arts Project and an Arthur Zankel Fellow at Columbia University's Teachers College, his work appears in a number of journals, and is featured on HBO, BET, NPR, *Upworthy* and *The New York Times.* www.adamfalknerarts.com www.dialogueartsproject.com

Malcolm Friend is a poet and CantoMundo fellow originally from the Rainier Beach neighborhood of Seattle, Washington, and an MFA candidate in Creative Writing at the University of Pittsburgh. His work has appeared or is forthcoming in publications such as *La Respuesta* magazine, the *Fjords Review's Black American Edition, The Acentos Review, Pretty Owl Poetry* and elsewhere.

Ross Gay is a gardener and teacher living in Bloomington, Indiana. His books include *Catalog of Unabashed Gratitude, Bringing the Shovel Down* and *Against Which.*

Maria Mazziotti Gillan is winner of the 2014 George Garrett Award for Outstanding Community Service in Literature from AWP, the 2011 Barnes & Noble Writers for Writers Award from Poets & Writers, and the 2008 American Book Award for her book, *All That Lies Between Us.* She is the Founder/Executive Director of the Poetry Center at Passaic County Community College, editor of the *Paterson Literary Review,* and director of the creative writing program/professor of English at Binghamton University-SUNY. She has published 20 books, including: *The Silence in an Empty House, Ancestors' Song* and *Girls in the Chartreuse Jackets.* www.mariagillan.com.

Brian Gilmore teaches law at Michigan State University. He is the author of three books of poetry, including *We Didn't Know Any Gangsters,* a 2014 NAACP Image Award nominee for poetry.

Keith Gilyard has been on the faculty of The Pennsylvania State University, University Park, since 1999. He is the author/editor of 17 books, including the memoir, *Voices of the Self* and the biography, *John Oliver Killens*, both American Book Award winners. His latest collection of poetry is *Wing of Memory*.

Veronica Golos is the author of *A Bell Buried Deep*, *Vocabulary of Silence* and *ROOTWORK*. She is the co-editor of the *Taos Journal of International Poetry & Art*, and poetry editor for the *Journal of Feminist Studies in Religion*.

Jaki Shelton Green is a 2009 Piedmont Laureate. Her work appears in *The Crucible, The African-American Review, Obsidian, Poets for Peace, Ms. Magazine, Essence, KAKALAK, Callaloo, Cave Canem African American Writers Anthology* and *The Pedestal Magazine*. She is the author of *Dead on Arrival, Masks, Conjure Blues, singing a tree into dance, Blue Opal (a play), breath of the song* and *Feeding the Light*.

Rachel Eliza Griffiths teaches at Sarah Lawrence College. A poet and visual artist, she is the author of *Miracle Arrhythmia, The Requited Distance, Mule & Pear* and *Lighting the Shadow*.

Minal Hajratwala is an award-winning author, poet, writing coach, and co-founder of The (Great) Indian Poetry Collective, devoted to publishing new poetic voices from global India.

Joy Harjo was born in Tulsa, Oklahoma and is a member of the Mvskoke Nation. Her award-winning books of poetry include, *How We Became Human- New and Selected Poems, The Woman Who Fell From the Sky, She Had Some Horses* and *For A Girl Becoming,*. She is the recipient of many awards, such as the New Mexico Governor's Award for Excellence in the Arts, the Lifetime Achievement Award from the Native Writers Circle of the Americas; and the William Carlos Williams Award from the Poetry Society of America. A musician as well as a poet, she has released four award-winning CDs of original music and in 2009 won a Native American Music Award (NAMMY) for Best Female Artist of the Year for Winding Through the Milky Way.

Niki Herd grew up in Cleveland and earned degrees in Creative Writing from the University of Arizona and Antioch University. Nominated twice for a Pushcart Prize, she is the recipient of fellowships from Cave Canem and the Virginia Center for the Creative Arts. Her work has been supported by the Astraea Foundation and the Arizona Commission on the Arts, and has appeared in several journals and anthologies. Her debut collection of poems, *The Language of Shedding Skin*, was a finalist for the Benjamin Saltman Prize chosen by Nick Flynn in 2010. In that same year, it was also a finalist for the Main Street Rag Poetry Award and was published by the press. She lives in Washington, DC.

Everett Hoagland has read his work to audiences in China, Africa, Latin America and all over the USA and has been regularly published for half a century. His two most recent books are the anthology *Ocean Voices* and *The Music & Other Selected Poems*. Former Poet Laureate of New Bedford, MA, he is Emeritus Professor at the University of Massachusetts Dartmouth and the recipient of the 2015 Langston Hughes Society Award.

Rashidah Ismaili is a writer of poetry, fiction, non-fiction and plays. She is a member of faculty for the MA and MFA Creative Writing at Wilkes University, Wilkes-Barre, PA. Her latest work of fiction is *Autobiography of the Lower East Side* published by North Hampton Press. She hosts Salon d' Afrique at her place in Harlem, a gathering of national and international artists and scholars.

Esther Iverem is an award-winning author, artist and activist. Her most recent book is *We Gotta Have It: Twenty Years of Seeing Black at the Movies*, 1986-2006. She is founder of SeeingBlack.com and a producer and host for WPFW Pacifica Radio in Washington, DC. www.estheriverem.com

Reuben Jackson lives in Winooski, Vermont. He is host of Vermont Public Radio's Friday Night Jazz, and a workshop leader with the Young Writers Project.

Patricia Spears Jones is a poet, playwright and cultural critic. She is author of four full-length collection, the most recent *A Lucent Fire: New & Selected Poems* (White Pine Press) and four chapbooks. Recipient of awards from the NEA, NYFA and the Foundation of Contemporary Arts. Originally from Arkansas, she lives and works in New York City.

Quincy Scott Jones is the author of *The T-Bone Series*. His work has appeared in the *African American Review* and *The Feminist Wire*. With Nina Sharma he co-created the *Nor'easter Exchange*: a multicultural, multi-city reading series.

Allison Joseph lives, writes, and teaches in Carbondale, Illinois, where she is on the faculty at Southern Illinois University. Her books include Soul Train (Carnegie-Mellon), *In Every Seam* (University of Pittsburgh), and *Trace Particles* (Backbone Press).

Douglas Kearney teaches at CalArts. His third poetry collection, *Patter*, was a finalist for the California Book Award in Poetry. *The Black Automaton* was a National Poetry Series selection.

Ruth Ellen Kocher is the author of six poetry collections: *Ending in Planes* (Noemi Press, 2014), *Goodbye Lyric: The Gigans and Lovely Gun* (Sheep Meadow Press, 2014), *domina Un/blued* (Tupelo Press, 2013), *One Girl Babylon* (New Issues Press, 2003), *When the Moon Knows You're Wandering* (New Issues Press, 2002), and *Desdemona's Fire* (Lotus Press, 1999).

Yusef Komunyakaa is the author of many distinguished books of poetry, including *Taboo, Dien Cai Dau, Warhorses, The Chameleon, Testimony* and *Neon Vernacular*, for which he received the Pulitzer Prize. His plays, performance art and libretti have been performed internationally and include *Saturnalia, Testimony* and *Gilgamesh*. He is a professor of creative writing at New York University.

Nile Lansana is a student at Jones College Prep in Chicago and a member of Rebirth Poetry Ensemble. He has been writing since the age of 10 and his work is featured in *The Breakbeat Poets: New American Poetry in the Age of Hip-Hop*.

Onam Lansana is a 16 year old poet. He is from the south side of Chicago. He has performed his work across the country. He has participated in the Louder Than a Bomb Poetry Slam for two years and the Brave New Voices Poetry Slam for one year. He was previously published in *The BreakBeat Poets: New American Poetry in the Age of Hip-Hop*. His work evaluates issues of race and culture in the United States.

Quraysh Ali Lansana is a faculty member of the Creative Writing Program of the School of the Art Institute. His books include *mystic turf, They Shall Run: Harriet Tubman Poems, The BreakBeat Poets: New American Poetry in the Age of Hip Hop* (with Kevin Coval and Nate Marshall) and *The Walmart Republic* (with Christopher Stewart).

Raina J. León is the author of three collections of poetry, *Canticle of Idols* (2008), *Boogeyman Dawn* (2014) and *sombra: dis(locate)* (2016). She is a co-founding editor *of The Acentos Review*, an online quarterly, international journal devoted to the promotion and publication of Latin@ arts. She is an assistant professor of education at Saint Mary's College of California.

Kenji C. Liu is author of *Map of an Onion*, national winner of the Hillary Gravendyk Poetry Prize. Among other places, his poetry appears in *American Poetry Review, Action Yes!, Asian American Literary Review*, Split This Rock's poem of the week series, several anthologies and a chapbook, *You Left Without Your Shoes*. He has received fellowships from Kundiman, VONA/Voices, Djerassi, and the Community of Writers.

Haki R. Madhubuti co-founded the quarterly *Black Books Bulletin* with Larry Neal, the Institute of Positive Education, the New Concept School, the Betty Shabazz International Charter School, the International Literary Hall of Fame for Writers of African Descent and the National Black Writers Retreat. His many award-winning books include, *Don't Cry, Scream, Groundwork: Selected Poems of Haki R. Madhubuti / Don L. Lee, Dynamite Voices I: Black Poets of the 1960s* and *Black Men: Obsolete, Single, Dangerous?*, as well as the anthology, *Million Man March/Day of Absence: A Commemorative Anthology*.

devorah major, poet in residence at San Francisco's Fine Arts Museums and a senior adjunct Professor at the California College of the Arts, served as Poet Laureate of San Francisco from 2002-2006. A novelist as well as a poet, her many books include *An Open Weave, Brown Glass Windows, street smarts, where river meets ocean* and *with more than tongue.*

Jamaal May is a Detroiter and the author of *Hum*, recipient of several honors and awards. Co-director of Organic Weapon Arts with Tarfia Faizullah, his poems have appeared in such publications as *Poetry, The New Republic, NYTimes.com* and *Best American Poetry* 2014 and 2015.

Tony Medina is professor of creative writing at Howard University. His books include *I and I, Bob Marley,* winner of the Paterson Prize for Books for Young People; *Broke on Ice; An Onion of Wars; The President Looks Like Me & Other Poems* and *My Old Man Was Always on the Lam,* a Paterson Poetry Prize finalist.

Kamilah Aisha Moon writes, teaches and lives in Brooklyn, NY. A Pushcart Prize winner and finalist for the Lambda Literary Award, she is published widely in journals and anthologies such as the *Harvard Review* and *Gathering Ground*. Moon is the author of *She Has a Name* (Four Way Books) and holds an MFA from Sarah Lawrence College.

Thylias Moss, Macarthur Fellow, 1996; Professor Emerita, 2015, working now for Thylias Moss Writing LLC, author of ten published books including *Tokyo Butter* and *Slave Moth*, with an 11th, *Wannabe Hoochie Mama Gallery of Realities RED DRESS Code*, new and selected. She is maker of poams and creator of "Limited Fork Theory" which she offers in the following websites to anyone who is able to access them: The Institute of 4orkological Studies; The Mid-Hudson Taffy Company; Lexicon 97. She is active on Facebook as Forker Gryle, and be sure to check out her video poams on her YouTube channel.

Ricardo Nazario y Colón is the author of *The Recital* and *Of Jíbaros and Hillbillies*. Co-founder of the Affrilachian Poets, he has studied at Fordham University, the University of Kentucky and Pace University. His work appears in numerous journals, including *Tidal Basin Review, Louisville Review, Aphros Review, BlazeVox*. Visit him at www.lalomadelviento.com or email him at kayuka@yahoo.com.

Marilyn Nelson was awarded the 2012 Frost Medal from the Poetry Society of America. In January 2013 she was elected a Chancellor of The Academy of American Poets. Her latest collection for young adults is *How I Discovered Poetry*, a memoir in verse with illustrations by Hadley Hooper. Her many distinguished titles include, *A Wreath For Emmett Till, Carver: A Life in Poems, A Wreath For Emmett Till, Faster Than Light*, winner of the Milton Kessler Poetry Award. Her latest collections, all published for young adults, are *How I Discovered Poetry, My Seneca Village*, and *American Ace*. Her many distinguished titles include *Carver: A Life in Poems, The Fields of Praise*, and *Faster Than Light*.

Rae Paris is Assistant Professor of Creative Writing at Michigan State University. Her writing appears in *The Common, Guernica, Dismantle, Solstice*, and other journals. Her work has been supported by the NEA, the Helene Wurlitzer Foundation, VONA, Hambidge, Atlantic Center for the Arts and Hedgebrook.

Bao Phi is the author of a *Sông I Sing*. A Vietnamese refugee, a single co-parent, and has been a performance poet and community organizer since the early 1990s, he has appeared on *Russell Simmons Presents Def Poetry* and a poem of his appeared in *Best American Poetry* (2006). He is the Program Director of the Loft Literary Center and remains active as a poet and community organizer.

Khadijah Queen is the author of *Conduit, Black Peculiar, Fearful Beloved* and *I'm So Fine: A List of Famous Men & What I Had On*. Her verse play, *Non-Sequitur*, won the 2014 Leslie Scalapino Award for Innovative Performance Writing. She is board chair for Kore Press and works as an editor for a finance company.

Camille Rankine is the author of *Incorrect Merciful Impulses* and the chapbook, *Slow Dance with Trip Wire*, selected by Cornelius Eady for the Poetry Society of America's 2010 New York Chapbook Fellowship. The recipient of a 2010 "Discovery"/*Boston Review* Poetry Prize, she is Assistant Director of the MFA Program in Creative Writing at Manhattanville College.

Ishmael Reed is the author of thirty titles including the acclaimed novel *Mumbo Jumbo*, as well as essays, plays and poetry. His award-winning books include, *The Freelance Pallbearers*; *The Terrible Threes*; *The Last Days of Louisiana Red*; *Yellow Back Radio Broke Down*; *Reckless Eyeballing*; *Flight to Canada*; *Japanese by Spring* and *Juice!* His most recent book is the bestselling, *The Complete Muhammad Ali*. He is publisher and editor of *Konch*.

Tennessee Reed is the author of seven poetry collections, a memoir and a novel. She has read her work around the continental United States, Alaska, Hawaii, England, the Netherlands, Germany, Switzerland, Israel and Japan. She currently has a poetry collection in manuscript as well as a short story. She is a photographer, the secretary of PEN Oakland and the managing editor of Konch Magazine.

Kim Roberts is the author of four books of poems, most recently *Fortune's Favor: Scott in the Antarctic* (Poetry Mutual, 2015). She edited the anthology *Full Moon on K Street: Poems About Washington, DC* (Plan B Press, 2010), and co-edits the journal*Beltway Poetry Quarterly* and the web exhibit *DC Writers' Homes*. Her website: http://www.kimroberts.org.

Metta Sáma is author of *le animal & other creatures, After "Sleeping to Dream"/After After* and *Nocturne Trio*. The founder of Artists Against Police Brutality/Cultures of Violence, she is Director of Center for Women Writers & Director of Creative Writing at Salem College.

Sonia Sanchez is the author of over 16 books including *Homecoming, We a BaddDDD People, Love Poems, I've Been a Woman, A Sound Investment and Other Stories, Homegirls and Handgrenades, Under a Soprano Sky, Wounded in the House of a Friend, Does Your House Have Lions?, Like the Singing Coming off the Drums, Shake Loose My Skin, Morning Haiku* and *I'm Black When I'm Singing, I'm Blue When I Ain't and Other Plays*. She was the first Presidential Fellow at Temple University and she held the Laura Carnell Chair in English at Temple University.

Jon Sands is the author of *The New Clean*. His work appears in *The New York Times* and *The Best American Poetry 2014*. He is co-founder of Poets in Unexpected Places and the interviews editor at *Union Station Magazine*. He is also a Youth Mentor with Urban Word-NYC, and runs a weekly creative writing workshop for adults at Bailey House in Harlem (an HIV/AIDS Service Center).

Danny Simmons is a noted visual artist, novelist and poet. His books include, *I Dreamed My People Were Calling but Couldn't Find My Way Home..., Deep in Your Best Reflection* and *The Brown Beatnik Tomes*. He is the creator and co-executive producer of the award-winning HBO show, *Russell Simmons Presents Def Poetry Jam*.

Marilyn Singer is the author of over 100 children's books, many of which are poetry collections. She lives in Brooklyn, NY and Washington, CT with her husband and several pets. Visit her web site: www.marilynsinger.net.

giovanni singleton is founding editor of *nocturnes (re)view of the literary* arts and the 2014-15 Visiting Assistant Professor in the creative writing programs at New Mexico State University. Her work has been exhibited in the Smithsonian Institute's American Jazz Museum, San Francisco's first Visual Poetry and Performance Festival, and on the building of Yerba Buena Center for the Arts. Her book *Ascension* received the 81st California Book Award Gold Medal.

Lynne Thompson is the author of two books of poetry, *Beg No Pardon* and *Start with a Small Guitar,* as well as the e-book, *Jezebels on the Loose.* She is reviews and essays editor of the journal, *Spillway.*

Venus Thrash holds an MFA from American University. She is the author of *The Fateful Apple*, which was long-listed for the 2015 PEN America Open Book Award. Her work has been published in *Beltway Quarterly*, *Torch*, and *Split This Rock*.

Askia M. Toure', poet, activist, Black Arts co-founder, co-wrote the SNCC Black Power Position Paper published in the New York Times, in 1966. He lives in Boston, MA.

Quincy Troupe, Professor Emeritus from the University of California, San Diego and editor of *Black Renaissance Noire* at New York University, is the author of 20 books, including *Errançities; Miles: the Autobiography*; *Earl the Pearl* with Earl Monroe; *The Pursuit of Happyness*, with Chris Gardner; and the editor of *James Baldwin: The legacy*. His awards include the Paterson Award for Sustained Literary Achievement, the Milt Kessler Poetry Award, three American Book Awards, the 2014 Gwendolyn Brooks Poetry Award and a 2014 Lifetime Achievement Award from Furious Flower. His work has been translated into over 30 languages.

Frank X Walker is the co-founder of the Kentucky based writing collective, the Affrilachian Poets and a Cave Canem Fellow. He is the author of eight volumes of poetry and recipient of numerous awards, including a Lannan Foundation Poetry fellowship. He is a professor in the department of English and the African American and Africana Studies Program at the University of Kentucky.

Jerry W. Ward, Jr., author of *THE KATRINA PAPERS: A Journal of Trauma and Recovery*, lives in New Orleans.

Afaa Michael Weaver was born in Baltimore in 1951. He is the recipient of the 2014 Kingsley Tufts Award. www.plumflowertrilogy.org.

Marvin K. White is an Oakland, California based poet, writer, M.Div. student, activist, Pastor Intern at Glide Memorial Church in San Francisco and Facebook Statustician. He is the author of four collections of poetry, *last rights, nothin' ugly fly, our name witness* and *status*.

Phillip B. Williams is a Chicago, IL native and the author of *Thief in the Interior* (Alice James Books 2016). A Cave Canem fellow, he is a recipient of a 2013 Ruth Lilly fellowship and currently serves as the 2015-2017 Creative Writing Fellow in poetry at Emory University.

L. Lamar Wilson is the author of *Sacrilegion*, 2012 Carolina Wren Press Poetry Series winner and 2014 Thom Gunn Poetry Award finalist, and co-author of *Prime*. Wilson's poems appear in *Callaloo, jubilat, The Los Angeles Review, Rattle, The 100 Best African American Poems*, and *Please Excuse This Poem: 100 New Poems for the Next Generation*.

Acknowledgments/Permissions

Abdul Ali, "Elegy" was originally published in *Trouble Sleeping* (New Issues Poetry& Prose, 2015). Reprinted by permission of Abdul Ali.

Ching-In Chen, "Manifesto of Shame" was first published in *Callaloo*.

Rita Dove, " 'Teach Us to Number Our Days' " from *Yellow House on the Corner* (Pittsburgh: Carnegie Mellon University Press, 1989). Reprinted with the permission of Rita Dove.

Adam Falkner, "The Definition of Privilege" first appeared in *Uncommon Core: Poems for the Living and Learning* (Red Beard Press, 2013). Reprinted by permission of Adam Falkner.

Ross Gay, "A Small Needful Fact" was first published on *Split This Rock*.

Keith Gilyard, "it's hard out here for a spirit" was originally published in *Wing of Memory* (Whirlwind Press, 2015). Reprinted with permission of Keith Gilyard.

Rachel Eliza Griffiths "Elegy" and "Anti Elegy" first published in *Lighting the Shadow* (Four Way Books, 2015)

Joy Harjo, "I Give You Back" was first published in *How We Became Human: New and Selected Poems: 1975 – 2001* (W.W. Norton and Company Inc., 2002). Reproduced with the permission of Joy Harjo.

"I Give You Back" copyright © 1983 by Joy Harjo from SHE HAD SOME HORSES by Joy Harjo. Used by permission of W.W. Norton and Company, Inc.

Quraysh Ali Lansana, "Statement on the Killing of Patrick Dorismond" was first published in *The Walmart Republic* (w/Christopher Stewart), Mongrel Empire Press, 2015.

Jamaal May, "The Gun Joke" originally published by *Indiana Review* (winner of the 2013 IR Prize).

Kamilah Aisha Moon, "The Emperor's Deer" first appeared in *Fjords Review*.

Marilyn Nelson, "Emmett Till's name still catches in my throat" was first published in *Carver: A Life in Poems* (Front Street, Boyds Mills Press, 2001). Reprinted with the permission of Marilyn Nelson.

"Emmett Till's Name Still Catches in My Throat" from A WREATH FOR EMMETT TILL by Emmett Till. Text copyright © 2005 by Marilyn Nelson. Reprinted by Permission of Houghton Mifflin Harcourt Publishing Company. All rights reserved.

Rae Paris, "Strangled*: Letter to A Young Black Poet" first appeared in Issue 117, *Transition Magazine: the Magazine of Africa and the Diaspora*.

Bao Phi, "8 (9)" is reprinted by permission from *Sông I Sing* (Coffee House Press, 2011).

Khadijah Queen, "Theory: Evidence of uncertain shifts" was previously published in *The Offing*.

Camille Rankine, "Survival Guide for Animals Born in Captivity" first appeared in *Apogee Journal*.

Ishmael Reed, "Red Summer" first appeared in *Konch*, 2015. Reprinted with the permission of Ishmael Reed.

Sonia Sanchez, "elegy (for MOVE and Philadelphia)" and "Philadelphia: Spring, 1985" was first published in *Under a Soprano Sky* (Africa World Press, 1987) Republished with the permission of Sonia Sanchez.

Lynne Thompson's "In America's Mirror" was first published in *Margie*. "Sonnet Consisting of One Law" was first published on Rattle. com. Both are reprinted with the permission of Lynne Thompson.

I would like to express my deepest gratitude to the following individuals for making this dynamic and necessary project happen: My publisher, Richard Krawiec, for his vision and commitment; Daniel Krawiec, for his exquisite design and attention to detail; my dear friend, Metta Sama, for her assistance in gathering work and her keen editorial eye; Thomas Sayers Ellis, for his percussive photo that graces the cover; and to all the fine poets who dedicated their creativity to this movement of witness.

— Tony Medina